SIDE BY SIDE

French & English

GRAMMAR

Third Edition

SIDE BY SIDE

French & English

GRAMMAR

Third Edition

C. Frederick Farrell Jr., PhD

New York   Chicago   San Francisco   Lisbon   London   Madrid   Mexico City
Milan   New Delhi   San Juan   Seoul   Singapore   Sydney   Toronto

To our students, who had questions

1 2 3 4 5 6 7 8 9 10 11 12 13 14 15 16 17   QDB/QDB   1 9 8 7 6 5 4 3 2

ISBN   978-0-07-178859-5
MHID   0-07-178859-X

e-ISBN 978-0-07-178860-1
e-MHID   0-07-178860-3

Library of Congress Control Number 2011937086

Interior design by Village Bookworks

McGraw-Hill products are available at special quantity discounts to use as premiums and sales promotions or for use in corporate training programs. To contact a representative, please e-mail us at bulksales@mcgraw-hill.com.

This book is printed on acid-free paper.

Contents

Preface

Side by Side French & English Grammar presents the essential elements of French grammar—usually covered in a high school program or in the first year of college French—"side by side" with their English counterparts. This comparative/contrastive approach allows students to build on what they already know, as they see the ways in which English and French are similar, and to avoid potential trouble spots.

Side by Side French & English Grammar has been used in both high school and college French classes, and even in some English classes for a few students who were having trouble in understanding their English grammar text. Its vocabulary is, for the most part, limited to the 1,500 most frequently used French words.

This book has been used as

1. a reference book for beginning students, for whom the standard works are too complex to be useful. This allows students a means for independent inquiry.

2. a means of quick review of material forgotten over the summer or material missed because of illness.

3. a means of helping a student in a new school catch up with the class.

4. a means of organizing or summarizing material presented in the primary text, especially for students whose learning style favors an "organized approach."

5. a means of providing a common background for talking about language with students who have studied English in different ways, so that their study of French will show them something about how language works, one of the expectations of many college language requirements.

6. an alternative method of explaining grammatical points in both English and French to relieve the classroom teacher of the task.

Special features of the book that students will find useful include

1. a standard format that introduces each part of speech and answers the most common questions about it.

2. Quick Check charts that allow students to express themselves with more confidence, since they can independently check their sentences against a model.

3. appendices that identify and summarize trouble spots, such as the differences between the forms of the relative and interrogative pronouns, and material for passive learning only, such as the literary tenses.

4. an exercise section that tests understanding of the main grammatical areas covered in the book, plus Using your French, a section new to this edition, that prepares students for communication in French.

We hope that this text will provide ways for students to increase their independent work and to adapt material to their own learning styles and situations.

Acknowledgments

I remain thankful to my colleagues, all now formerly of the University of Minnesota–Morris: Professors Emeriti W. D. Spring and Jeffrey L. Burkhart, who read the English and French sections, respectively, of the original version of *Side by Side French & English Grammar,* for their patience, humor, and helpful suggestions; Professors Emeriti Sheryl James and Brigitte Weltlman-Aron (French) and Dorothy Barber, Jeanne Purdy, and James Gremmels (English), who read subsequent editions; the staff of the UMM Computer Center; and David Stillman, who compiled the exercise section.

The development of this book was supported in part by a grant from the Educational Development Program of the University of Minnesota.

Introduction

This book grew out of a series of supplements to a French grammar text. Its purpose is to help you learn French more easily.

Many students have had trouble with foreign languages because they have not looked carefully enough, or critically enough, at their own. Struggles with your own language took place at such an early age that you have forgotten the times when it seemed difficult. Now it seems perfectly natural to you, and it is hard to adapt to different ways of expressing ideas.

The material in this book has been classified and arranged to show you English and your new language "side by side." You may be surprised at how many grammatical elements are similar in the two languages.

Information that is the same for both English and French is usually not repeated on facing pages. If you find that a section is omitted under the French, look to your left and find it on the English page. The English meaning of a French example is usually on the left-hand page, too.

Why grammar?

People can speak, read, or write their native language, at least to a reasonable degree, without studying formal grammar (the rules governing how we say, change, and arrange words to express our ideas). Just by being around other speakers, we hear millions of examples, and the patterns we hear become a part of us. Even babies start with correct basic patterns (subject-verb-object), even though words may be missing or incorrect: "Me wants cookie!"

Knowledge of grammar helps a great deal, though, in testing new and more complex words or patterns and in analyzing one's writing to discover where a sentence went wrong or how it could be more effective. Sometimes, "It sounds right (or wrong)" won't help.

All of the explanations in this book reflect standard English or French. You may sometimes think, "I don't say that!" The important word here is "say." We often ignore some rules in conversation, or even in informal writing such as friendly letters. When you are writing an important paper or giving a speech, however, you may want to use the standard form in order to make the best possible impression. You will also find that knowing grammar will help you in your study of language.

In learning a foreign language, grammar is necessary because it tells you how to choose the right word—or the right form of a word that you are using for the first time. It is not the way that you acquired your native language as a child, but it is an efficient way for adults who want to express more complex ideas and do not want to make any more mistakes than absolutely necessary.

Grammar saves you time and prevents many mistakes by guiding you in your choices.

1

Introducing languages

A short history of English

What we now know as England was settled in the fifth and sixth centuries A.D. by Germanic tribes like the Angles, the Saxons, and the Jutes—all speaking related, but distinct, dialects. Later, in the ninth century, Scandinavian invaders came, bringing their languages, which also contributed to English. Political power determined the centers of learning, which contained the literature of continental Europe, written in Latin, as well as contributions of the inhabitants of Britain. By the ninth century, the primary center was in Wessex, due to the Viking invasions in the north, and so the West Saxon dialect became standard as Old English. It was heavily inflected, with endings on nouns to show many cases and on verbs to show time and person.

This was the language current in 1066, when William the Conqueror, from the province of Normandy in what is now France, won the battle of Hastings and became ruler of England. The natives knew no French; William and his followers did not speak Old English. For a long time, each group continued to speak its own language, but gradually they merged. Since the governing group spoke French, we often find that words for work, home, and ordinary things come from Old English, while words for leisure or artistic goods come from French.

Wamba, the jester in Sir Walter Scott's *Ivanhoe,* made a joke about this, saying that cows and pigs were Anglo-Saxon while the peasants took care of them, but became French (beef and pork) when they were ready to be eaten. In the same way, "house" looks and sounds like the German word *Haus,* but "mansion" looks like the French word for "house," *maison.*

English often uses several words with a similar meaning, with the more elegant word frequently being of French origin. For example, instead of "give," we may say "donate," which is like the French *donner*; instead of "mean," we may say "signify," from French *signifier.*

Latin, the language of the church and therefore of learning in general throughout all Europe, also had an influence on English. Around 1500, English absorbed about 25 percent of known Latin vocabulary. English, therefore, is basically a Germanic language, but one to which large portions of French and Latin were added.

Since the French also borrowed from Latin in the Renaissance, the languages have many words in common, but they are not the everyday words. Compare the following.

GERMANIC ROOT (COMMON)	FRENCH ROOT (ELEGANT)	LATIN ROOT (LEARNED)
ask	*question*	*interrogate*
goodness	*virtue*	*probity*
better	*improve*	*ameliorate*
rider	*cavalier*	*equestrian*

Knowing basic French words may help you recognize the meaning of new English words that you encounter.

A short history of French

French is one of the Romance languages, like Spanish, Italian, and others, that have developed from Latin. When Julius Caesar invaded Gaul (now France) in the first century B.C., he encountered different peoples with different languages. When they tried to learn Latin from the Roman soldiers—who were not language teachers—they learned "mistakes," and they also pronounced the words a little differently, because they continued to use the familiar sounds of their own languages. They spoke with a foreign accent. Other peoples, like those in northern Italy and Spain, did the same thing.

This continued until the "Latin" of different countries evolved into different, though related, languages. Now, while you can guess at words and even forms and rules in a Romance language, based on your knowledge of one of them, a speaker of Spanish cannot be understood by a speaker of French, and vice versa. As in English, Latin words were added to French in the sixteenth century to form a "learned" language. These words were generally used only by educated people and so have not changed over the years, as have the ones with a 2,000-year history.

Many French people are much more protective of their language than we are of English, and they are very careful about how they use it. In fact, there is an *Académie française*, which prescribes the standard language. Because of this concern for preservation and correctness, French changes more slowly than English. However, all languages change, and the trend is toward less inflection. Distinctions that seem to be too hard or unnecessary die out.

Over the centuries, different languages have eliminated different linguistic elements. For example, in Latin and other older languages, every noun had gender, number, and case (which indicated its function in a sentence). In fact, modern German still uses all three grammatical distinctions.

In English, we pay little attention to grammatical gender, but nouns still have number (singular and plural) and an additional case (the possessive), while pronouns also have an objective case; the functions of other cases are expressed by word order and prepositions. French no longer has cases for nouns, but it does have grammatical gender and number. You will notice other instances in which French and English differ. Comparing languages is interesting, because it points out the important elements in each language. Let's examine the forms of a common masculine noun in Germanic languages.

	MODERN GERMAN		OLD ENGLISH		MODERN ENGLISH
	SINGULAR	PLURAL	SINGULAR	PLURAL	SINGULAR/PLURAL
SUBJECT	*der König*	*die Könige*	*se cyning*	*tha cyningas*	*the king/kings*
GENITIVE	*des Königs*	*der Könige*	*thoes cyning*	*thara cyninga*	*the king's/kings'*
DATIVE	*dem König*	*den Königen*	*thaem cyninge*	*thaem cyningum*	*to the king/kings*
OBJECTIVE	*den König*	*die Könige*	*thone cyning*	*tha cyningas*	*the king/kings*

Declension (listing all the case forms of a noun) in German is further complicated by having feminine and neuter nouns whose definite articles and endings are different from the example above, as well as irregular nouns, which have different forms altogether. Adjectives in modern German also have different endings for each gender and case.

Now, let's compare Latin, French, and English forms in the present tense conjugation of the verb "to have."

LATIN		MODERN FRENCH		MODERN ENGLISH	
habeo	*habemus*	*j'ai*	*nous avons*	*I have*	*we have*
habes	*habetis*	*tu as*	*vous avez*	*you have*	*you have*
habet	*habent*	*il a*	*ils ont*	*he has*	*they have*

The endings in Latin are so distinctive that it is not necessary to indicate the subject. This is also true of modern languages like Spanish and Italian. The *h* is often not pronounced in many European languages, and never in standard French. *V* and *b* are similar sounds, and in Spanish they are almost identical. Modern English is the least inflected of the modern languages referenced here, French is next, then Italian, Spanish, and German.

Parts of speech

Introducing the parts of speech

Both English and French words are categorized by parts of speech. You may have learned these in elementary school without understanding their usefulness. They are important, because different rules apply to the different categories. In your own language, you do this naturally, unless the word is new to you. You know to say *one horse, two horses*, adding an *-s* to make the noun *horse* plural. You do not try to apply a noun's rule to a verb and say *I am, we ams*; instead, you say *we are*. People learning a foreign language sometimes use the wrong set of rules, however, because all of the forms are new, so nothing "sounds wrong." To avoid this kind of mistake, learn the part of speech when you learn a new vocabulary word.

Parts of speech help you identify words, so that even if a word is used in several ways (and this happens in both English and French), you can determine the French equivalent. For instance, *that* can be

1. a conjunction.

   > I know **that** Mary is coming.
   > Je sais **que** Marie vient.

2. a demonstrative adjective.

   > **That** person is impossible.
   > **Cette** personne est impossible.

3. a pronoun.

   > I didn't know **that**.
   > Je ne savais pas **cela**.

When you know the parts of speech, the fact that a word is used several ways in English won't cause you to choose the wrong one in French.

Following is a list of the parts of speech. The parts are described (1) in traditional definitions, (2) by the forms that identify them, and (3) by their functions (as structural linguists think of them).

Nouns

1. Names or words standing for persons, places, things, or abstract concepts

   > *John*
   > *man*
   > *Paris*
   > *city*
   > *table*
   > *justice*

2. Words that become plural by adding *-s* or *-es* (in addition to a few other ways)

   > *book ~ books*
   > *fox ~ foxes*
   > *child ~ children*

3. Words that function as subjects, objects, or complements

   > **John** is here.
   > She read the **book**.
   > There is **Mary**.

Pronouns

1. Words that substitute for nouns

   > John is already here. Have you seen **him**?

2. Words that are used when no noun is identified

   > **It** is raining.
   > **They** say . . .
   > **You** never know.

3. Words that serve the same function as nouns

   > **He** is here.
   > **He** loves **her**.
   > There **it** is.

Adjectives

1. Words that modify, limit, or qualify a noun or pronoun

    dumb
    red
    serious
    happy

2. Words that may be inflected (may change form) or may be preceded by *more* or *most* to make comparisons

    dumb ~ dumber ~ dumbest
    *serious ~ **more** serious ~ **most** serious*

Verbs

1. Words that express action, existence, or state of being

    speak
    learn
    run
    be
    have
    feel

2. Words that may be inflected to show person (*I **am** ~ he **is***), time (*I **sing** ~ I **sang***), voice (*I **write** ~ it **is written***), and mood (*if I **am** here ~ if I **were** you*)

Adverbs

1. Words that modify verbs, adjectives, or other adverbs by telling how, when, where, or how much

    *We'll come **soon**.*
    *It's **really** big.*
    *They do it **very** well.*

2. Words that can show comparison between verbs (as adjectives do for nouns)

    soon ~ sooner ~ soonest
    *rapidly ~ **more** rapidly ~ **most** rapidly*

Prepositions

1. Words that express place, time, and other circumstances and show the relationship between two elements in a sentence

    at
    for
    in
    of
    on
    to

2. Words that are not inflected (never change form)

3. Words that have a noun or pronoun as their object

    ***in** a minute*
    ***of** a sort*
    ***on** it*

These groups are called prepositional phrases.

Conjunctions

1. Coordinating conjunctions (for example, *and*, *but*, and *so*) connect words, phrases, or clauses that are grammatically equivalent.

    *John **and** Mary*
    *on the table, **but** under a napkin*
    *I had no money, **so** I stayed at home.*

2. Subordinating conjunctions (for example, *if*, *because*, and *when*) connect subordinate clauses to the main clause of a sentence.

    ***When** you see it, you will believe me.*

Interjections

1. Exclamations

    Hey!
    Wow!

2. Words that can be used alone or in sentences

    Darn!
    ***Oh**, Mary, is it true?*

3

Nouns

Definition	See page 6.
Forms	English nouns are considered to have gender, number, and case.

GENDER Masculine or feminine gender is used only for someone or something that is male or female.

> *man*
> *woman*
> *bull*
> *tigress*

All other nouns are neuter. Gender makes no difference in English except when there are two forms for one noun (for example, *actor* and *actress*) or when the nouns are replaced by pronouns (for example, *he, she, it*).

NUMBER Most nouns add *-s* or *-es* to the singular form to form the plural.

> *train ~ trains*
> *box ~ boxes*

Some nouns have irregular plural forms.

> *mouse ~ mice*
> *man ~ men*
> *child ~ children*

CASE There is only one extra case in English: the possessive, or genitive. It is formed by adding *-'s* to a singular noun or *-'* to a plural noun ending in *-s*.

> **Mary's** *book*
> *the* **book's** *cover*
> *the* **books'** *covers*

The possessive case can often be ignored, and *of* used instead, although this form is less common when a person is involved.

> *Kant's theories → the theories* **of Kant**
> *the book's pages → the pages* **of the book**

Nouns are often preceded by determiners (see page 16).

> **a** *book,* **the** *book,* **my** *book,* **two** *books*

Uses	The three most common uses of nouns are as subjects, objects, and complements (see page 14).

SUBJECT	**Mrs. Dupont** *is French.*
APPOSITIVE	*Mrs. Dupont, a French* **woman**, *is visiting us.*
DIRECT OBJECT OF A VERB	*He has a* **pencil**.
INDIRECT OBJECT OF A VERB	*She gave the hat to* **John**.
OBJECT OF A PREPOSITION	*We are in the* **room**.
COMPLEMENT	*It is a valuable* **book**.
ADJECTIVE	*I have my* **history** *textbook.*

CONTINUED ON PAGE 12 ▶

Introducing nouns

Definition See page 6.

Forms French nouns are considered to have gender and number, but not case.

GENDER All nouns in French are either masculine or feminine; there are no neuter nouns. When you learn a French noun, you must also learn whether it is masculine or feminine.

The gender of nouns is very important in French, since their determiners and the adjectives accompanying them must be of the same gender. If a noun is preceded by *le* or *un*, it is masculine; *la* and *une* designate a feminine noun. *L'* is used before a word beginning with a vowel or a silent (mute) *h* to make it easier to say. *L'* does not tell you which gender the word is.

NUMBER Most French nouns add *-s* to form the plural, but they also have a plural article, because the final *-s* is not pronounced. *Les* replaces both *le* and *la* and is used for both masculine and feminine nouns. *Des* is the plural form for *un* and *une*.

Some common French nouns have irregular plural forms. For example, nouns ending in *-al* usually have a plural ending in *-aux*, and those ending in *-eau* or *-eu* have plurals ending in *-eaux* or *-eux*, respectively.

> *le journal ~ les journaux*
> *l'eau ~ les eaux*
> *le lieu ~ les lieux*

Words ending in *-s, -x,* or *-z* do not change in the plural.

> *un cours ~ des cours*
> *un prix ~ des prix*
> *le nez ~ les nez*

Proper nouns never change form.

> *les Duval*

CASE French nouns do not have different cases. Possession is indicated by the preposition *de,* plus an article if one is needed.

> *les théories **de Kant***
> *les pages **du livre***

French nouns are often preceded by determiners (see page 16).

> ***un** livre, **le** livre, **mon** livre, **deux** livres*

Uses Nouns are used in the same way in French and English. Compare the following sentences with the English sentences on the opposite page.

> ***Madame Dupont** est française.*
> *Mme Dupont, une **Française**, nous rend visite.*
> *Il a un **crayon**.*
> *Elle a donné le chapeau à **Jean**.*
> *Nous sommes dans la **pièce**.*
> *C'est un **livre** précieux.*
> *J'ai mon texte **d'histoire**.*

Rarely is a French noun used alone as an adjective; a phrase, usually with *de,* is used.

CONTINUED ON PAGE 13 ▶

English Introducing nouns (continued)

Types There are several ways to classify nouns. Following are two important ones.

1. Common vs. proper

    Common nouns are applied to a class of individuals. They begin with a lowercase letter.

    > student
    > country
    > cat
    > language

    Proper nouns name a specific individual within a class. They begin with a capital letter.

    > Miss Jones
    > France
    > Kitty
    > English

2. Countable vs. mass

    Countable nouns can be counted.

    > one pencil
    > two sharks
    > three engineers

    Mass nouns cannot be separated into individuals—they cannot be counted.

    > salt
    > weather
    > sadness

Types French nouns may be classified as follows.

1. Common vs. proper

   For the most part, French is the same as English in this classification, but there are a few important differences. Nouns for languages, days of the week, and months are common nouns in French and do not require a capital letter.

English	*l'anglais*
Monday	*lundi*
October	*octobre*

2. Countable vs. mass

   This classification follows the same principle in French as in English. To use them, however, frequently requires a partitive construction in French (see page 18).

Introducing subjects and objects

Subjects

Subjects are most frequently nouns or pronouns. The subject of a verb is the person or thing that *is* something or *is doing* something.

> **Mary** and **I** are here.
> **John** speaks French.
> Are **they** (the textbooks) *arriving today?*

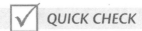 **QUICK CHECK**

Ask yourself: *Who* is here? *Who* speaks French? *What* is arriving?

Answer: the subject

In normal word order, the subject comes before the verb. The subject is often, but not always, the first word in a sentence or clause.

Subject complements

Subject complements are words or phrases that define, or complete an idea about, the subject.

> Mr. White is a **professor**.
> Jeanne and Alice are **Americans**.

Direct objects

Some systems of grammar refer to direct objects as "object complements." The name matters less than the ability to recognize their important function. Direct objects are usually nouns or pronouns that directly receive the verb's action. In normal word order, the direct object comes after the verb.

> Mary likes **John**. She likes **him**.
> The professor is giving a **test**. He is giving **it**.

 **QUICK CHECK**

Ask yourself: *Who* is liked? *What* is being given?

Answer: the direct object

Indirect objects

Indirect objects are usually nouns or pronouns that are indirectly affected by the verb's action. They indicate *to* whom or *for* whom something is done.

> *Speak* **to me**!

Verbs of communication often have implied direct objects, as in *Tell me (the news)*. These objects are sometimes expressed in other languages.

COMBINATIONS Some verbs (for example, *give*, *tell*, and *buy*) can have more than one object. In addition to a direct object, there can be an indirect object. Counting the subject, there can be three nouns or pronouns with different functions, even in a short sentence.

> **Robert** *gives* **the book**   **to Alice**.
> SUBJECT   DIRECT OBJECT   INDIRECT OBJECT

> **Robert** *gives* **Alice**   **the book**.
> SUBJECT   INDIRECT OBJECT   DIRECT OBJECT

> **He** *gives* **it**   **to her**.
> SUBJECT   DIRECT OBJECT   INDIRECT OBJECT

Notice that the two possible word orders have no effect on which object is direct and which is indirect. The word order in English simply determines whether or not the word *to* is used.

 **QUICK CHECK**

To analyze the sentences above, ask yourself: *Who gives?*

Answer: *Robert* or *he* (the subject)

Who or *what* is given?

Answer: *the book* or *it* (the direct object)

To/for whom / to/for what is it given?

Answer: *Alice* or *her* (the indirect object)

Objects of prepositions

All prepositions must have objects (see page 7). These objects come immediately after the preposition.

> *on the* **table** *~ on* **it**
> *after* **Peter** *~ after* **him**

In questions and relative clauses in English (see page 72), this rule is often ignored, and the preposition is used alone at the end of the sentence.

> **To whom** *did you give it?*
> → **Whom** *did you give it* **to?**

The first sentence is considered standard English. French uses the same patterns as standard English.

Problems with direct and indirect objects

English and French verbs with the same meaning usually take the same kind of object, but not always. The exceptions must be learned as vocabulary items. See the chart below for examples.

Comparison of objects in English and French

DIRECT OBJECT IN ENGLISH	INDIRECT OBJECT IN FRENCH
He **obeys** his parents.	*Il* **obéit à** *ses parents.*
He **phones** Ann.	*Il* **téléphone à** *Anne.*
I **am answering** the letter.	*Je* **réponds à** *la lettre.*
Mary always **asks** John.	*Marie* **demande** *toujours* **à** *Jean.*

OBJECT OF A PREPOSITION IN ENGLISH	DIRECT OBJECT IN FRENCH
I **am paying for** the tickets.	*Je* **paie** *les billets.*
Monica **is looking for** the book.	*Monique* **cherche** *le livre.*
Michael **is waiting for** the teacher.	*Michel* **attend** *le professeur.*
The student **listens to** the teacher.	*L'étudiant* **écoute** *le professeur.*

English Introducing determiners

Definition   Determiners are words that introduce nouns and their adjectives. They usually come first in a noun phrase.

> *the* red book
> *a* tall boy
> *each* window
> *several* students

Types   Many kinds of words can serve as determiners: definite articles, indefinite articles, partitives, numbers, and general words like *each, either,* and *several.* Some types of adjectives (possessives, demonstratives, and interrogatives) can also be determiners; these are discussed in Chapter 5.

Forms   The **definite article** is always written *the,* but it is pronounced like *thee* before words beginning with a vowel or silent *h* (*the book* vs. *the apple, the hour*). The **indefinite article** is *a* or *an* in the singular, *some* in the plural. *An* is used before words beginning with a vowel or silent *h.* Other forms of determiners do not change their spelling or pronunciation.

Uses   DEFINITE ARTICLES *The* indicates a specific noun.

> *The* book (the one you wanted) *is on the table.*

INDEFINITE ARTICLES *A/an* refers to any individual in a class.

> I see *a* boy (not a specific one).

OTHER DETERMINERS The use of other determiners is governed by the meaning.

> *some* boys
> *few* boys
> *several* boys
> *eight* boys

Forms **DEFINITE ARTICLES** The form of the French definite article depends on the gender and number of its noun and on whether it begins with a vowel or, often, an *h*. In a vocabulary list or dictionary, a word beginning with *h* that takes the same determiner as a word beginning with a consonant is marked with an asterisk (*) or some other symbol (for example, *le *héros*).

	BEFORE A CONSONANT	BEFORE A VOWEL AND MANY *h*s
MASCULINE SINGULAR	*le* jour	*l'homme* (BUT *le* héros)
FEMININE SINGULAR	*la* télévision	*l'étudiante*
PLURAL	*les* jours	*les hommes* (links as a *z* sound)
	les télévisions	*les étudiantes*

These forms can also be combined with the prepositions *à* and *de* (see page 73).

INDEFINITE ARTICLES The indefinite article agrees with its noun in gender and number, just as the definite article does. However, because the indefinite article ends in a spoken consonant, it does not change its spelling before a vowel. Instead, in speaking, we link the *n* or *s* sound to the beginning of the next word.

	BEFORE A CONSONANT	BEFORE A VOWEL AND MANY *h*s
MASCULINE SINGULAR	*un* jour	*un ami* (links as an *n* sound)
FEMININE SINGULAR	*une* télévision	*une amie*
PLURAL	*des* jours	*des amis* (links as a *z* sound)
	des télévisions	*des amies*

PARTITIVES Partitives are normally formed by the preposition *de* plus the appropriate definite article.

> *du* pain
> *de la* glace
> *de l'eau*
> *des* livres

There are four situations in which *de* is used alone.

1. Normally after an expression of quantity

> *beaucoup de* vin
> *tant de* gens

When the noun following *de* refers to a specific item or group, the definite article is used.

> *bien **des** gens*
> *la plupart **des** étudiants*
> *beaucoup **des** étudiants de cette classe* ("many of the students in this class")

2. After a negative

> *Il **n'y** a **pas d'**argent dans mon sac.*

3. After an expression including *de*

> *J'**ai besoin d'**amis.*

4. Before a plural adjective

> *Jean et Jeanne sont **de bons** enfants.*

CONTINUED ON PAGE 18 ▶

OTHER DETERMINERS Every determiner must be learned as a separate vocabulary item. Some determiners change spelling for gender or number; be sure to check as you learn new words.

> *plusieurs*
> *chaque*
> *tout/toute/tous/toutes*

Uses **Definite articles** are used

1. before a specific noun, as in English.

2. before a noun used in a general sense.

*Je déteste **la** télévision.*	I hate television (generally speaking).
***La** guerre est mauvaise.*	War (in general) is bad.

3. before many kinds of nouns that take no article in English.

LANGUAGES	***l'**anglais*
QUALITIES	***la** beauté*
COUNTRIES	***la** France*
TITLES	***le** général*
MODIFIED PROPER NAMES	***le** vieux Paris*

Indefinite articles are used

1. for the number "one."

> ***un** étudiant, **une** étudiante*

2. for any member of a group or category.

> *Paul a **un** bon professeur.*

Partitives are used to express part of a whole. English, which does not make this distinction, usually places no determiner before the noun.

***L'**argent est utile.*	Money (in general) is useful.
*J'ai **de l'**argent.*	I have (some) money.

Since English typically uses the single word *money* in these cases, we have to stop and think. Do we mean *all* money or money *in general* (and therefore use only the definite article in French), or do we mean just *some* money (what we have today, for example), in which case we use the partitive. Following are additional examples.

*J'aime **la** glace. **La** glace est bonne.*	I like ice cream. (All) ice cream is good.

Much as I like it, however, I can consume only a *part* of this whole quantity.

*Je voudrais **de la** glace, s'il vous plaît.*	I'd like ice cream, please.

The definite article is used to refer to a group as a whole.

***Les** étudiants à l'université sont intelligents.*	(All) students at the university are intelligent.

But it is not used to refer to a *part* of a group.

*Il y a **des** étudiants dans la salle de classe.*	There are students in the classroom.

OTHER DETERMINERS Most other French determiners are used as they are in English. See Appendix B.

Pronouns

Definition See page 6.

Forms Like nouns, English pronouns have gender, number, and case, but further distinctions can be made. They also show person.

PERSON English distinguishes three persons. **First person** is the one who is speaking (*I, me, we, us*). **Second person** is the one being spoken to (*you*). **Third person** is the one being spoken about (*he, him, she, her, it, they, them*). Both pronouns and verbs are listed according to person.

GENDER Some, but not all, pronouns can be distinguished by gender. *I* can refer to either a man or a woman. *She*, however, is always feminine, *he* always masculine, and *it*, even if it refers to an animal, is always neuter.

NUMBER Each of the three persons may be either singular or plural.

CASE Pronouns show more cases than nouns: the subjective (for example, *I* and *she*), the possessive (for example, *my/mine* and *her/hers*), and the objective (*me* and *her*). These are discussed below, under Uses.

Uses Personal pronouns have the same functions as nouns.

1. Subject

    She *is here.*

2. Direct object

    *I like **them**.*

3. Indirect object

    *I am giving **him** the book.*

4. Object of a preposition

    *The question is hard for **me**.*

5. Complement

    *It is **she** who is speaking.*

Types There are several types of pronouns.

1. Personal (page 22)

2. Possessive (page 26)

3. Reflexive/reciprocal (page 28)

4. Disjunctive (page 30)

5. Relative (page 32)

6. Demonstrative (page 36)

7. Interrogative (page 38)

French Introducing pronouns

Definitions, forms, and uses are the same for French and English pronouns. However, there are three important differences to be aware of.

1. In French, the personal pronoun for *you* has two forms in the singular—the familiar (*tu*) and the formal (*vous*). The plural form is always *vous*.

   Tu is used to address the following.

   > A member of your family
   > Yourself
   > A close friend
   > A fellow student or colleague
   > A child (under age 13)
   > An inferior (sometimes as an insult)
   > An animal
   > God

   Vous is used for everyone else. Be careful: Unless the case is clear (for example, a dog or a small child), use *vous* and allow the French person to suggest using *tu*. A complication is that this use is largely a personal preference; some people never use *tu* except for family members, children, and animals.

2. *On* (the equivalent of the English pronoun *one*) is listed with personal pronouns because it is used very frequently in French—much more so than *one* in American English, which tends to use *you* or *they* for an indefinite subject (for example, *It's true, you know* or *They say that . . .*).

   On may replace any personal pronoun to avoid being too personal. Circumstances indicate what is being referred to.

On est fâché.	One is angry.

   On est invité à… is more modest than "We got an invitation to . . .".

   However, regardless of the pronoun replaced, *on* always takes a third-person singular verb.

3. There is no neuter gender in French: *Il* replaces masculine things as well as people, and *elle* replaces feminine ones. In the third-person plural, *ils* is used both for groups of masculine people or things and for mixed groups; *elles* is used only for all-feminine groups.

 **Personal pronouns**

Subject pronouns (see page 14)

	SINGULAR	PLURAL
FIRST PERSON	*I*	*we*
SECOND PERSON	*you*	*you*
THIRD PERSON	*he, she, it, one* (indefinite)	*they*

John gives a present. → **He** *gives it.* (third-person singular)
Mary and I arrive. → **We** *arrive.* (first-person plural)

Direct object pronouns (see page 14)

	SINGULAR	PLURAL
FIRST PERSON	*me*	*us*
SECOND PERSON	*you*	*you*
THIRD PERSON	*him, her, it, one*	*them*

He sees **me**, *and I see* **you**.
You found **them**.

CONTINUED ON PAGE 24 ▶

French Personal pronouns

Subject pronouns (see page 14)

In French, a subject pronoun must always be of the same gender and number as the noun that it replaces.

	SINGULAR	PLURAL
FIRST PERSON	*je*	*nous*
SECOND PERSON	*tu*	*vous*
THIRD PERSON	*il, elle, on*	*ils, elles*

Note the lowercase *j* of *je* in the first-person singular.

Direct object pronouns (see page 14)

	SINGULAR	PLURAL
FIRST PERSON	*me*	*nous*
SECOND PERSON	*te*	*vous*
THIRD PERSON	*le, la*	*les*

*Il **me** voit, et je **vous** vois.*
*Vous **les** avez trouvés.*

The final letter/vowel of a singular form elides (is dropped) before a vowel or silent *h*.

*Il **m'**aime.*
*Elle **l'**adore.*

For the third person, choosing the correct pronoun is easy if you remember that the pronoun is the same as the definite article; in the following example, the definite article and pronoun are *le*.

*Je cherche **le** livre. → Je **le** cherche.*

POSITION Except in affirmative commands, an object pronoun in French is placed directly before the conjugated verb or infinitive of which it is the object.

*Il **me** voit. Je **vous** vois.*	He sees me. I see you.
*Je cherche le livre. → Je **le** cherche.*	I am looking for it.
Pierre aime lire les lettres.	
*→ Pierre aime **les** lire.*	Peter likes to read them.

The object pronoun is also placed directly before the verb in a question or a negative sentence.

*Avez-vous les billets? → **Les** avez-vous?*	Do you have them?
*Je n'ai pas les billets. → Je ne **les** ai pas.*	I don't have them.
*N'a-t-il pas les billets? → Ne **les** a-t-il pas?*	Doesn't he have them?

The only exception is in affirmative commands.

Donnez le pain à Marie.	
*→ Donnez-**le** à Marie.*	Give it to Mary.

In negative commands, the pronoun is placed before the verb.

Ne donnez pas le pain à Marie.	
*→ Ne **le** donnez pas à Marie.*	Don't give it to Mary.

For more information about pronouns with commands, see page 109.

CONTINUED ON PAGE 25 ▶

Indirect object pronouns (see page 14)

	SINGULAR	PLURAL
FIRST PERSON	*(to/for) me*	*(to/for) us*
SECOND PERSON	*(to/for) you*	*(to/for) you*
THIRD PERSON	*(to/for) him, her, it, one*	*(to/for) them*

*They send the letter **to us**.*
*He writes **her** a letter.*
*I bought a dress **for her**.*
*I got **them** a ticket.*

Objects of prepositions (see page 15)

After a preposition, English uses the same form of the pronoun as for direct objects.

Be careful with compound pronoun subjects or objects. These remain in the same case as that for a single subject or object.

***I** am French. **She** and **I** are French.*
*This is between **us**. This is between **you** and **me**.*
*Give it to **them**. Give it to **him** and **her**.*

WORD ORDER When there are two pronoun objects in English, the direct object comes before the indirect object.

*He shows **it** to **them**.*

When a noun and a pronoun are used together, word order can vary.

He shows ***the book***   ***to them**.*
       DIRECT OBJECT   INDIRECT OBJECT

He shows ***them***   ***the book**.*
       INDIRECT OBJECT   DIRECT OBJECT

 **Personal pronouns** (continued)

Indirect object pronouns (see page 14)

In French, the indirect object is often used where English would use a preposition plus object.

	SINGULAR	PLURAL
FIRST PERSON	*me*	*nous*
SECOND PERSON	*te*	*vous*
THIRD PERSON	*lui*	*leur*

Indirect object pronouns are placed before the verb, just as direct object pronouns are.

*Je **lui** ai acheté une robe.*   I bought her a dress.
                                              OR I bought a dress for her.

*Je **leur** ai procuré un billet.*   I got them a ticket.
                                              OR I got a ticket for them.

Objects of prepositions (see page 15)

Most prepositions require the disjunctive pronouns in French (see page 31). However, two pronouns replace both a preposition and its object.

En replaces *de* plus a noun.

*Il a besoin **d'argent**. → Il **en** a besoin.*   He needs some.
***En** a-t-elle?*   Does she have any?

Y replaces *à* plus a noun or any place preposition plus a noun.

*Je pense souvent **à mon lycée**.*
     *→ J'**y** pense souvent.*   I often think about it.
*Le billet est **dans mon sac**.*
     *→ Le billet **y** est.*   The ticket is there.

WORD ORDER Some French verbs often have more than one pronoun object.

*Il **le leur** montre.*   He shows it to them.

The order of pronouns before a verb is determined as follows.

1. Remember "1-2-3." A first-person pronoun comes before a second-person pronoun, and a second-person pronoun comes before a third-person pronoun.

2. If there are two third-person objects, the direct object comes before the indirect object.

3. *Y* and *en* always come last, and in that order.

> ✓ *QUICK CHECK*

NORMAL FRENCH WORD ORDER

SUBJECT + *me*   + *le* + *lui* + *y* + *en* + VERB
                   te   *la*   *leur*
                   nous   *les*
                   vous

Remember that *me, te, le, la* become *m', t', l'* before a vowel or silent *h*.

CONTINUED ON PAGE 27 ▶

 Possessive pronouns

Definition   A possessive pronoun replaces a possessive adjective (or a noun in the possessive) plus a noun.

> It's **my book**. → It's **mine**.
> It's **Anne's car**. → It's **hers**.

Forms   Possessive pronouns have person and number; in the third-person singular, they also have gender. They do not have case, that is, they have the same form no matter what function they perform in a sentence.

	SINGULAR	PLURAL
FIRST PERSON	*mine*	*ours*
SECOND PERSON	*yours*	*yours*
THIRD PERSON	*his, hers, its, one's*	*theirs*

If you know the person, gender, and number of the possessor (*Mary* in the example below), there is only one choice for the pronoun (in this example, *hers*).

> *You have your book; where is **Mary's** book (**her** book)?*

To avoid repeating *book,* it is replaced along with the possessive noun or adjective in front of it. Since *Mary's* (or *her*) is third-person singular feminine, *hers* is the correct pronoun.

> *You have your book; where is **hers**?*

 **Personal pronouns** (continued)

In affirmative commands, the objects *follow* the verb. The direct object comes before the indirect object, regardless of person.

*Donnez-**le-moi**!*	Give it to me!
*Montrez-**les-lui**!*	Show them to him/her!

✓ **QUICK CHECK**

ORDER FOR AFFIRMATIVE COMMANDS ONLY

	DIRECT OBJECT		INDIRECT OBJECT		
			moi (m')		
	le (l')		*toi (t')*		
VERB +	*la (l')*	+	*nous*	+ *y* + *en*	
	les		*vous*		
			lui		
			leur		

Moi, toi, le, la become *m', t', l'* before a vowel or silent *h*.

Possessive pronouns

Forms In French, possessive pronouns have person and number as in English, but they also have gender changes for the singular forms. "Person" means the possessor, while gender and number are determined by what is owned.

***le** livre de Marie*	Mary's book	***les** chemises de Jean*	John's shirts
***son** livre*	her book	***ses** chemises*	his shirts
le sien	hers	***les siennes***	his

Even though *Marie* is female, the possessive pronoun is masculine singular (***son** livre*, ***le sien***), because *livre* is masculine. Likewise, although *Jean* is male, *chemises* is feminine plural and therefore requires a feminine plural pronoun (***ses** chemises*, ***les siennes***).

	SINGULAR	PLURAL
FIRST PERSON	*le mien, la mienne, les miens, les miennes*	*le nôtre, la nôtre, les nôtres*
SECOND PERSON	*le tien, la tienne, les tiens, les tiennes*	*le vôtre, la vôtre, les vôtres*
THIRD PERSON	*le sien, la sienne, les siens, les siennes*	*le leur, la leur, les leurs*

 **Reflexive/reciprocal pronouns**

Definition   Reflexive pronouns are pronoun objects or complements that refer to the same person(s) or thing(s) as another element in the sentence, usually the subject.

Forms

	SINGULAR	PLURAL	RECIPROCAL
FIRST PERSON	*myself*	*ourselves*	*each other/one another*
SECOND PERSON	*yourself*	*yourselves*	*each other/one another*
THIRD PERSON	*himself, herself, itself, oneself*	*themselves*	*each other/one another*

Uses   Reflexive pronouns are used as objects of verbs and prepositions.

Types   A reflexive pronoun is normally used only when the subject acts directly on himself/herself or does something for himself/herself directly.

> **Paul** *cut* **himself**.
> **I** *told* **myself** *it didn't matter.*

Occasionally, reflexive pronouns are used idiomatically.

> **They** *always enjoy* **themselves**.

For mutual or reciprocal action, *each other* or *one another* is used. This expression does not change form.

> **They** *congratulated* **each other**.
> **You** *two saw* **each other** *last night.*

Reflexive pronouns can function as direct or indirect object pronouns.

> **They** *saw* **each other**.
> **We** *talked to* **each other** *yesterday.*

In English, reflexive and reciprocal objects are often omitted.

> **We** **talked** *yesterday.* (*To each other* is understood.)

Sometimes, a construction is used that requires no object.

> **Paul** **got hurt**. (*Hurt himself* is understood.)

However, consider the following sentence.

> *We washed this morning.*

If you have not heard the rest of the conversation, the meaning is ambiguous. The sentence may have either of the following meanings.

> *We washed ourselves (got washed).*
> *We washed our clothes (did the laundry).*

Reflexive/reciprocal pronouns

Forms The forms of French reflexive/reciprocal pronouns are the same as the forms of the direct and indirect object pronouns, except for the third person.

	SINGULAR	PLURAL
FIRST PERSON	*me (m')*	*nous*
SECOND PERSON	*te (t')*	*vous*
THIRD PERSON	*se (s')*	*se (s')*

Reflexive/reciprocal pronouns are placed in the same position in a sentence as object pronouns.

Uses These pronouns are used as objects (either direct or indirect) of the verb (see page 14). They can be either reflexive or reciprocal, meaning either "self" or "each other."

> *Ils **se** parlent.*   They are talking to themselves.
>   OR They are talking to each other.

If the meaning is not clear, words can be added, especially *l'un(e) (à) l'autre, les un(e)s les autres.*

> *Ils **se** regardent **les un(e)s les autres**.*
> DIRECT OBJECT

> *Ils **se** parlent **les un(e)s aux autres**.*
> INDIRECT OBJECT

French uses many more reflexives than English, because transitive verbs must have objects in French. Contrast the following sentences.

> *Nous arrêtons l'auto.*   We stop the car.
> *Nous **nous** arrêtons.*   We stop.

Some French verbs are only reflexive. Even though the reflexive pronoun is used in French, it is not translated in English.

> *Je **m'**en vais.*   I'm leaving.
> *Ils **s'**amusent.*   They are having a good time.

Following is the present tense of the reflexive verb *s'arrêter.*

	SINGULAR	PLURAL
FIRST PERSON	*je m'arrête*	*nous nous arrêtons*
SECOND PERSON	*tu t'arrêtes*	*vous vous arrêtez*
THIRD PERSON	*il/elle s'arrête*	*ils/elles s'arrêtent*

English Disjunctive pronouns

Definition A disjunctive pronoun is not attached to a verb. (*Disjunctive* means "not joined.") It is used alone or as an extra word to give special emphasis or to intensify an impression.

Forms and uses The form of a disjunctive pronoun depends on its use.

1. Used alone, the disjunctive pronoun is in the subjective case (if required) in formal English, and in the objective case for informal use.

   Who's there? **I**. (formal; *I am* is understood)
   Me. (informal)

2. As an intensifier, the reflexive pronoun is normally used.

   I'll do it **myself**!
   He told me so **himself**.

3. Sometimes, we merely raise our voices for emphasis.

   You *do it!*

French Disjunctive pronouns

Forms   The disjunctive pronouns have special forms in French.

	SINGULAR	PLURAL
FIRST PERSON	*moi*	*nous*
SECOND PERSON	*toi*	*vous*
THIRD PERSON	*lui, elle, soi* ("oneself")	*eux, elles*

Uses   Disjunctive pronouns may be used

1. alone.

   Qui est là? **Moi!**

2. as a complement after *c'est*.

   C'est **toi!**

3. as an intensifier.

   Moi, *je vais le faire.* OR *Je vais le faire,* **moi.**   **I**'m going to do it.

4. with *même* for emphasis.

   Il me l'a dit **lui-même.**   He told me so **himself**.

5. after prepositions and conjunctions.

   Après nous, *le déluge.* (Madame de Pompadour)
   Paul est plus grand **que toi.**
   Chacun **pour soi.**   Every man **for himself**.

6. in compound subjects.

   Jean et moi, *nous y allons.*

7. in affirmative commands.

   *Donnez-***moi** *votre billet.*

 **Relative pronouns**

Definition   Relative pronouns begin a relative clause. They refer to a noun, called the antecedent, and usually come directly after that noun.

Forms   Relative pronouns have the following forms in English.

	SUBJECT	OBJECT	POSSESSIVE	INDIRECT OBJECT/PREPOSITIONAL OBJECT
PERSON	*who/that*	*whom/that*	*whose*	*to/by whom*
THING	*which/that*	*which/that*	*whose/*	*to/by which*
			of which	*where* (for place prepositions)
				when (for time prepositions)

The correct pronoun is determined by the following factors.

1. Whether the antecedent is a person or a thing

2. The function of the pronoun in the clause

3. For subjects and objects, whether the clause is restrictive or nonrestrictive

   A **restrictive clause** defines the noun. *That* is used, and the clause is not set off by commas.

   *The book **that** you just read is world-renowned.*

   Without the clause, you would not know which book is meant. It is an essential definition.

   A **nonrestrictive clause** describes the noun, rather than defines it. It is not necessary to form a complete sentence. *Who, whom,* or *which* is used, and the clause is set off by commas.

   *Madame Bovary, **which** the class is going to read, is very famous.*

   The relative clause could be eliminated, and the sentence would still make sense. It is a nonessential description.

Uses   Relative pronouns have several uses.

1. They introduce clauses that give additional information about the antecedent.

2. They allow you to join two short sentences to make your writing smoother and to avoid repetition.

   Mrs. Dubois came yesterday. Mrs. Dubois is an expert pianist.
   → *Mrs. Dubois, **who** is an expert pianist, came yesterday.*

3. They can be subjects, direct objects, indirect objects, possessives, or objects of a preposition in the relative clause.

4. They are inflected only for case, not for person or number. Their form depends on their function in the clause.

   The function of the antecedent in the main clause has no effect on the form of the relative pronoun.

French Relative pronouns

Forms Relative pronouns have the following forms in French.

	SUBJECT	OBJECT	PREPOSITIONAL OBJECT	OTHER
PERSON	*qui*	*que*	*qui/lequel*	*dont*
THING	*qui*	*que*	a form of *lequel*	*dont* *où* ("where" or "when")

Remember to use contractions with *à* and *de*, for example, *duquel* (see page 73).

Unlike English, French does not use different pronouns to distinguish between restrictive and nonrestrictive clauses.

> *Le livre **que** vous venez de lire est célèbre dans le monde entier.*
> Madame Bovary, ***que** la classe va lire, est très célèbre.*

Relative pronouns are often omitted in English.

> *That's the man I saw yesterday!*

French does not allow this.

> *C'est l'homme **que** j'ai vu hier.*

All relative pronouns must have antecedents. If there isn't one, *ce* is supplied.

> *He didn't come, which surprised me.* (*which* = subject)

There is no antecedent for *which*, so *ce* plus a relative pronoun is used.

> *Il n'est pas venu, ce **qui** m'a surpris.*

If the relative pronoun had been *que* or *dont*, *ce que* or *ce dont* would have been used.

A relative pronoun can take any form of the verb in its clause. This is also true of English, but many people do not follow this practice.

> *C'est moi **qui suis** anxieux.*   It is I who am worried.
> *Ce sont nous **qui arrivons**.*   We are the ones who are coming.

This can cause problems, because relative pronouns (in English and French) often look the same as interrogatives (for example, *who?* and *what?*), which always take a verb in the third person.

> *Qui **est** anxieux? Moi.*   Who is worried? I am.
> *Qui **arrive**? Nous.*   Who is coming? We are.

Mr. Smith *is **an excellent cook**.*		**Mr. Smith** *made **these pies**.*	
SUBJECT	COMPLEMENT	SUBJECT	DIRECT OBJECT

1. Find the repeated element. → *Mr. Smith*
2. Find the function of the repeated element in the second sentence, which will become the relative clause. → the subject
3. Choose the relative pronoun. → *who* (person, subject)
4. Copy the first sentence through the antecedent. → *Mr. Smith . . .*
5. Put in the correct relative pronoun, in this case, *who.* → *Mr. Smith, who . . .*
6. Copy the relative clause. → *Mr. Smith, who made these pies . . .*
7. Copy the rest of the first sentence. Leave out any parts represented by the relative pronoun. → *Mr. Smith, who made these pies, is an excellent cook.*

Other examples follow.

> *The ten books are on the table. I am reading them.*
> *The ten books **that** I am reading are on the table.*

> > *That* is used because it
> >
> > 1. is the object of *am reading* in the clause (no commas).
> > 2. refers to a thing.
> > 3. is restrictive (defines which ten books).

> *Mr. Jones died today. I saw him yesterday.*
> *Mr. Jones, **whom** I saw yesterday, died today.*

> > *Whom* is used because it
> >
> > 1. is the object of *I saw* (with commas).
> > 2. refers to a person.
> > 3. is nonrestrictive. (You already know who Mr. Jones is. This merely gives an extra fact about him.)

> *The student is asleep. I am speaking to that student.*
> *The student **to whom** I am speaking is asleep.*

> > *To whom* is used because it
> >
> > 1. is the indirect object (no commas).
> > 2. refers to a person.
> > 3. is restrictive (defines which student).

> *The old house is falling down. I lived in that house as a child.*
> *The old house **where** (in which) I lived as a child is falling down.*

> > *Where* is used because it
> >
> > 1. replaces a place preposition plus noun object (no commas).
> > 2. refers to a thing. (*In which* is also correct.)

> *The woman lives in New York. I took her coat.*
> *The woman **whose** coat I took lives in New York.*

> > *Whose* is used because it
> >
> > 1. is possessive (no commas).
> > 2. refers to a person.
> > 3. is restrictive (defines which woman).

French How to analyze relative pronouns

The important considerations are function in the clause and word order.

> **M. Smith** est **un excellent chef**.
> SUBJECT   COMPLEMENT

> **M. Smith** a fait **ces tartes**.
> SUBJECT   DIRECT OBJECT

1. Find the repeated element. → *M. Smith*
2. Identify the function of the repeated element in the second sentence, which will become the relative clause. → the subject
3. Choose the relative pronoun. → *qui*
4. Copy the first sentence through the noun phrase to be described. → *M. Smith…*
5. Put in the relative pronoun (with preposition, if any) to replace the second *M. Smith*. → *M. Smith, qui…*
6. Copy the rest of the second sentence (now a relative clause). → *M. Smith, qui a fait ces tartes,…*
7. Copy the rest of the first sentence. → *M. Smith, qui a fait ces tartes, est un excellent chef.*

Try this with other sentences. Follow the same steps until they feel natural.

> *Les dix livres sont sur la table. Je les lis.*
> *Les dix livres que je lis sont sur la table.*

> *M. Jones est mort aujourd'hui. Je l'ai vu hier.*
> *M. Jones, que j'ai vu hier, est mort aujourd'hui.*

> *L'étudiant est endormi. Je parle à cet étudiant.*
> *L'étudiant à qui je parle est endormi.*

> *La vieille maison s'écroule. Je vivais dans cette maison dans ma jeunesse.*
> *La vieille maison où je vivais dans ma jeunesse s'écroule.*
>   (*Dans laquelle* may also be used.)

> *La dame habite à New York. J'ai pris le manteau de cette dame.*
> *La dame dont j'ai pris le manteau habite à New York.*

This may seem complicated, requiring a lot of thought. That is because people usually use many short sentences when speaking. Relative clauses are used mainly to vary written style—when you have time to think, cross something out, and write it in a different way.

Definition   Demonstrative pronouns point out someone or something.

Forms   There are four forms of the demonstrative pronoun in English.

SINGULAR	PLURAL
this (one)	*these*
that (one)	*those*

Uses   These pronouns distinguish only between what is near (*this, these*) and far (*that, those*) and between singular and plural. No changes are made for gender or case.

> *I can't decide which of the chairs to buy.*
> **This one** *is lovely, but* **that one** *is comfortable.*
> **This** *is lovely, but* **that** *is comfortable.*

French Demonstrative pronouns

Forms There are four forms of the demonstrative pronoun in French.

	SINGULAR	PLURAL
MASCULINE	*celui*	*ceux*
FEMININE	*celle*	*celles*

Uses Demonstrative pronouns replace a demonstrative adjective plus its noun.

> **ce** *monsieur* OR **cet** *homme* → **celui**
> **cette** *dame* OR **cette** *image* → **celle**
> **ces** *hommes* → **ceux**
> **ces** *dames* → **celles**

In French, demonstrative pronouns are never used alone—something must follow to explain them.

1. *-Ci* or *-là*. These distinguish between near (*-ci*) and far (*-là*).

   Ceux-ci *sont bons, mais* **ceux-là** *sont*   These are good, but those are better.
   meilleurs.

   These affixes are also used to indicate "former" and "latter." Since the one "nearest" to the demonstrative pronoun is the last one mentioned, *celui-ci* means "the latter" and *celui-là* means "the former."

   Voilà Jean et Marc. **Celui-ci** *(Marc) est français, mais* **celui-là** *(Jean) est américain.*

2. A prepositional phrase

   Voici ma composition et **celle de Marie**.   Here is my composition and Mary's.

3. A relative clause

   Voici **celui que j'aime**.   Here is the one I like.

 QUICK CHECK

Notice that the form of the demonstrative pronoun is made up of the pronoun *ce* plus the disjunctive pronoun that would be used for that noun.

DEMONSTRATIVE ADJECTIVE + NOUN	DISJUNCTIVE PRONOUN	DEMONSTRATIVE PRONOUN
ce monsieur	*lui*	*celui*
cette dame	*elle*	*celle*
ces étudiants	*eux*	*ceux*
ces étudiantes	*elles*	*celles*

Definition Interrogative pronouns ask a question.

Forms Interrogative pronouns have different forms for people and things. The pronoun referring to people, *who,* is also inflected for case.

	PEOPLE	THINGS
SUBJECT	*who?*	*which?* *what?*
OBJECT	*whom?*	*which?* *what?*

No change is made for number. *Who?/whom?* and *what?* can refer to one or more than one.

Uses The interrogative pronouns in English are used in the following ways.

1. Person as subject

   Who *is coming? John.* OR *The Smiths.*

2. Thing as subject

   What *is going on? A riot.*

3. Person as direct object

   Whom *did you see? John.*

4. Thing as direct object

   What *are you doing? My homework.*

5. Person as indirect object*

   To whom *are you speaking? To Mary.*

6. Person as object of a preposition

   With whom *are you going? With Jean-Luc.*

7. Thing as object of a preposition

   What *are you thinking* **about**? *About the music.*

As an interrogative pronoun, *which?* relates to choice. It can simply be *which?*, used in the singular or plural, or *which one(s)?*

   Here are two books. **Which (one)** *do you want?*
   There are many good shops in town. **Which (ones)** *do you like best?*

---

*To or for signals the indirect object. (To review the indirect object, see page 14.)

 Interrogative pronouns

Forms
Interrogative pronouns are confusing in both English and French because the forms are used for other purposes, but they are more complex in French because, in most cases, you have a choice of two forms.

Short forms

	SUBJECT	OBJECT	OBJECT OF A PREPOSITION
PERSON	*qui* ***Qui** est là?*	*qui* ***Qui** regardez-vous?*	*qui* *À **qui** parlez-vous?*
THING	—	*que* ***Que** faites-vous?*	*quoi* ***De quoi** avez-vous besoin?*

Long forms

These interrogatives are made up of three parts: an interrogative pronoun + *est-ce* + a relative pronoun. The first part indicates if it refers to a person or thing; the last part indicates if it is a subject or object; the middle part, *est-ce*, indicates that the subject and verb are in normal word order.

Uses
The interrogative pronouns in French are used in the following ways.

1. Person as subject

   ***Qui** arrive?* OR ***Qui est-ce qui** arrive? Jean.* OR *Les Smith.*

2. Thing as subject

   ***Qu'est-ce qui** arrive? Une émeute.*

3. Person as direct object

   ***Qui** avez-vous vu? **Qui est-ce que** vous avez vu? Jean.*

4. Thing as direct object

   ***Que** faites-vous?* OR ***Qu'est-ce que** vous faites? Mes devoirs.*

5. Person as indirect object

   *À **qui** parlez-vous? À Marie.*

6. Person as object of a preposition

   ***Avec qui** allez-vous? Avec Jean-Luc.*

7. Thing as object of a preposition

   *À **quoi** pensez-vous? À la musique.*

 QUICK CHECK

	INTERROGATIVE PRONOUN		RELATIVE PRONOUN
PERSON AS SUBJECT	*qui*	+ *est-ce* +	*qui*
PERSON AS OBJECT	*qui*	+ *est-ce* +	*que*
THING AS SUBJECT	*qu'*	+ *est-ce* +	*qui*
THING AS OBJECT	*qu'*	+ *est-ce* +	*que*

CONTINUED ON PAGE 40 ▶

Choice interrogatives

Another kind of interrogative pronoun relates to choice: *Which one(s)?* These forms, which agree in gender and number with the noun they replace, are made up of the definite article + the interrogative adjective.

	SINGULAR	PLURAL
MASCULINE	*lequel*	*lesquels*
FEMININE	*laquelle*	*lesquelles*

These interrogatives offer a choice between possibilities.

> *Voici deux livres.* **Lequel** *voulez-vous?*
> *Il y a beaucoup de bonnes boutiques en ville.* **Lesquelles** *préférez-vous?*

5

Adjectives

English Introducing adjectives

Definition See page 7.

Forms Some English adjectives are invariable, while others change form. These changes depend on adjective type. The types are discussed separately below.

Uses Adjectives are primarily used as

1. modifiers of nouns or pronouns.

2. complements of either the subject or an object.

An adjective's function determines its position in a sentence.

1. As a modifier, an adjective usually comes before the noun or pronoun that it modifies.

*Buy **that small white house**.*
        ADJECTIVES   NOUN

*Buy the **blue**   one.*
        ADJECTIVE PRONOUN

2. As a modifier of an indefinite pronoun, an adjective follows the pronoun.

***Something**   terrible is happening.*
INDEFINITE PRONOUN   ADJECTIVE

3. As a subject complement, an adjective follows the verb *to be* or the linking verb and describes the subject.

*Mrs. Duval **is**   happy.*
        FORM OF *to be* ADJECTIVE

*They **seem**   pleased.*
        LINKING VERB ADJECTIVE

4. As an object complement, an adjective follows the direct object noun or pronoun.

*That made **the exam hard**.*
        NOUN   ADJECTIVE

*We considered **him**   crazy.*
        PRONOUN ADJECTIVE

Types Each of the following adjective types is discussed separately below.

1. Descriptive (page 44)

2. Proper (a kind of descriptive adjective) (page 48)

3. Limiting (includes demonstratives, possessives, indefinites, interrogatives, numbers, and determiners) (page 48)

Forms An adjective in French agrees in gender and number with the noun it modifies. If an adjective describes a mixed group of nouns (masculine and feminine), the adjective is masculine plural.

Uses As in English, French adjectives are used as modifiers and complements, but their position in a sentence is different (see page 45).

 Descriptive adjectives

Definition Descriptive adjectives describe a noun or pronoun.

Forms Many of these adjectives may be inflected to show comparison.

French Descriptive adjectives

Forms Descriptive adjectives normally add *-e* to form the feminine and *-s* to form the plural. The masculine singular form is the one listed first in vocabularies and dictionaries.

	SINGULAR	PLURAL
MASCULINE	*grand*	*grands*
FEMININE	*grande*	*grandes*

However, there are several groups of adjectives with irregular forms. (Note the corresponding examples in the table at the bottom of this page.)

1. Adjectives ending in silent *-e* in the masculine do not add another *-e* to form the feminine.

2. Adjectives ending in *-s* or *-x* do not change for the masculine plural.

3. Adjectives ending in *-eux* change to *-euse* in the feminine and do not change for the masculine plural.

4. Adjectives ending in *-f* change to *-ve* in the feminine.

5. Adjectives ending in *-eil, -el, -il, -ien,* or *-on* double the final consonant before adding *-e*.

6. Adjectives ending in *-ier* change to *-ière* in the feminine.

7. Adjectives ending in *-al* change to *-aux* in the masculine plural.

8. Some adjectives have an alternative masculine form to use before words beginning with a vowel and many words beginning with *h* to make pronunciation easier. The feminine is formed from the alternative masculine.

9. Some adjectives are completely irregular.

	SINGULAR		PLURAL	
TYPE	MASCULINE	FEMININE	MASCULINE	FEMININE
1	*facile*	*facile*	*faciles*	*faciles*
2	*français*	*française*	*français*	*françaises*
3	*heureux*	*heureuse*	*heureux*	*heureuses*
4	*vif*	*vive*	*vifs*	*vives*
5	*bon*	*bonne*	*bons*	*bonnes*
6	*fier*	*fière*	*fiers*	*fières*
7	*familial*	*familiale*	*familiaux*	*familiales*
8	*vieux* (*vieil*)	*vieille*	*vieux*	*vieilles*
	fou (*fol*)	*folle*	*fous*	*folles*
	beau (*bel*)	*belle*	*beaux*	*belles*
9	*blanc*	*blanche*	*blancs*	*blanches*

CONTINUED ON PAGE 45 ▶

French · Descriptive adjectives (continued)

WORD ORDER Normally, a descriptive adjective in French follows the noun it modifies. First, you say what you are talking about (for example, *une maison*), then you describe it (for example, *une maison blanche*).

Some common adjectives, however, are placed before the noun (for example, *une grande maison, une petite voiture*). Most adjectives of this kind fit into one of four groups, along with their opposites, according to what they are describing: **Size, Handsomeness, Age, Goodness** ("SHAG").

Size	*court*	*long*
	grand	*petit*
	haut	*bas*
	gros	*mince*
Handsomeness	*beau/joli*	*laid/vilain*
Age	*vieux*	*jeune*
Goodness	*bon*	*mauvais/méchant*
		pauvre ("pitiful," not "poor" in the sense of "penniless")

Some adjectives, including some of those above, can occur in both positions. If an adjective is meant literally, it tends to follow the noun; if its meaning is figurative, it precedes the noun.

un **grand** homme	a great man
un **homme** grand	a tall man
une **ancienne** église	a former church
une église **ancienne**	an old church
un **pauvre** homme	a man to be pitied
un homme **pauvre**	a man with no money
une **chère** amie	a dear friend
une robe **chère**	an expensive dress

English Comparison of adjectives

Definition The three degrees of comparison are positive, comparative, and superlative.

Forms English forms comparisons in the following ways.

1. Regular comparisons add -*er* and -*est* to short adjectives, sometimes with a minor change in spelling.

   *short ~ short**er** ~ short**est***
   *pretty ~ pret**tier** ~ pret**tiest***

2. Longer adjectives are compared by using *more* and *most,* or the negatives *less* and *least.*

   *determined ~ **more** determined ~ **most** determined*
   *obvious ~ **less** obvious ~ **least** obvious*

3. Some adjectives have irregular comparisons.

   good ~ better ~ best
   bad ~ worse ~ worst

4. Adjectives that cannot be compared include absolutes, which are by definition superlative. Uniqueness and perfection cannot be brought to a higher degree.

   unique
   perfect

5. When a comparison is made, several words may introduce the second element: *than, in,* and *of all.*

   COMPARATIVE *He is taller **than** I (am).*
   SUPERLATIVE *He is the tallest boy **in** the class. He is the tallest **of all** my students.*

If an adjective is already in the comparative, *more* is not added. Greater contrast may be expressed by words like *much* or *more.*

   ***much** smaller*
   ***much** more difficult*

Forms French forms comparisons in the following ways.

1. Regular French adjectives form the comparative with *plus* ("more"), *aussi* ("as" in the sense of equal), or *moins* ("less") plus the adjective.

   grand ~ **plus** *grand* ~ **aussi** *grand* ~ **moins** *grand*

2. Superlatives are formed with the definite article plus the comparative (for example, *le plus grand* and *la moins petite*).

   un **grand** *garçon* ~ *un* **plus grand** *garçon* ~ **le plus grand** *garçon*
   un bus **rapide** ~ *un bus* **moins rapide** ~ *le bus* **le moins rapide**

   The adjective remains in the same position, whether it is positive, comparative, or superlative.

   J'achète une **grande** *maison.*
   J'achète une **plus grande** *maison.*
   J'achète **la plus grande** *maison de la ville.*

3. The most common irregular comparisons are the following.

   bon ~ *meilleur* ~ *le meilleur*
   mauvais ~ *pire* ~ *le pire*

4. Adjectives that cannot be compared include absolute adjectives, which are by definition supcrlative.

   unique
   parfait

   Since uniqueness and perfection cannot be brought to a higher degree, *le/la/les plus* cannot be used with them.

5. When a comparison is made between two elements, *que* or *de* is used to link them.

COMPARATIVE	*Jean est plus grand* **que** *Marie.*
SUPERLATIVE	*Marie est la plus grande* **de** *sa famille.*

 QUICK CHECK

COMPARATIVE CONSTRUCTION WITH (1) *les hommes,* **(2)** *les femmes,*
AND (3) *être intelligents*

NOUN 1	+ VERB +	COMPARATIVE	+ ADJECTIVE	+ *que* +	NOUN 2
Les hommes	*sont*	*plus*	*intelligents*	*que*	*les femmes.*
		aussi			
		moins			

SUPERLATIVE CONSTRUCTION WITH (1) *Carole,* **(2)** *la classe,* **AND (3)** *être diligent*

NOUN 1 +	VERB +	SUPERLATIVE	+ ADJECTIVE +	*de* +	NOUN 2
Carole	*est*	*la plus*	*diligente*	*de*	*la classe.*

Make sure that the adjective agrees with the noun or pronoun it modifies.

English Proper adjectives

Definition   A proper adjective is a descriptive adjective formed from a proper noun (see page 12).

NOUN	ADJECTIVE
Rome	*Roman*
Shakespeare	*Shakespearean*

Forms   In English, both proper nouns and their adjectives are capitalized. Sometimes, their forms are indistinguishable.

NOUN	ADJECTIVE
the French	*the French people*

English Limiting adjectives

Definition   A limiting adjective does not add to your knowledge of a noun; instead, it directs you toward the right one by limiting the choices. The following examples show the types of limiting adjectives.

DEMONSTRATIVE	***this*** chapter (not another one)
POSSESSIVE	***his*** book (not hers)
INTERROGATIVE	***whose*** coat? (its specific owner)
INDEFINITE	***some*** people (but not others)
ORDINAL NUMBER	the ***second*** lesson (not the first)

Each of these types of limiting adjectives are discussed separately.

English Demonstrative adjectives

Definition   Demonstrative adjectives point out which of a group is/are the one(s) that you are referring to.

Forms   These adjectives have the same forms as the demonstrative pronouns (see page 36) and distinguish in the same way between near and far and between singular and plural.

	SINGULAR	PLURAL
NEAR	*this*	*these*
FAR	*that*	*those*

There is no agreement in person, gender, or case. The demonstrative adjective precedes its noun.

This *woman is talking to* ***that*** *man.*
These *little boys hate* ***those*** *dogs.*

French Proper adjectives

Forms In French, proper adjectives are formed from proper nouns, but they are not capitalized.

NOUN	ADJECTIVE
les Français	*le peuple français*

French Limiting adjectives

See the discussion on the opposite page.

French Demonstrative adjectives

Forms A demonstrative adjective agrees with the noun it modifies in gender and number.

	SINGULAR	PLURAL
MASCULINE	*ce* (*cet*)	*ces*
FEMININE	*cette*	*ces*

Uses The near/far distinction made in English does not arise in French unless there is a possibility of confusion. Then, *-ci* or *-là* is added to the noun to make the distinction.

> **Cette** *femme parle à* **cet** *homme.*
> **Ces** *petits garçons détestent* **ces** *chiens-***là**.

English Possessive adjectives

Definition Possessive adjectives modify a noun by telling to whom or what it belongs.

Forms These adjectives indicate the person, number, and gender (in the third-person singular) of the *possessor*.

	SINGULAR	PLURAL
FIRST PERSON	*my*	*our*
SECOND PERSON	*your*	*your*
THIRD PERSON	*his, her, its, one's*	*their*

The adjectives do not tell anything about the person or thing that is possessed.

> **Mr. Dupont's** *son* → **his** *son* (third-person singular masculine)
> **Mrs. Dupont's** *son* → **her** *son* (third-person singular feminine)
> **the Duponts'** *son* → **their** *son* (third-person plural)

Uses The possessive adjective is always used with the noun.

> **my** *mother*
> **our** *child*
> **your** *turn*

If the noun is omitted, a pronoun must be used (for example, *mine, ours,* or *yours*) (see page 26).

English Interrogative adjectives

Definition Interrogative adjectives ask a question about limitation.

Forms These adjectives have case in English.

1. Subject and object cases: *which? what?*

2. Possessive case: *whose?*

These forms are invariable.

Uses Interrogative adjectives are used

1. to ask a question.

> SUBJECT **What** *assignment is for today?*
> OBJECT **Which** *class do you have at 10 o'clock?*
> POSSESSIVE **Whose** *coat is this?*

2. in an exclamation.

> **What** *a pretty house!*
> **What** *a job!*

 # Possessive adjectives

Definition French possessives are adjectives, so they agree in gender and number with the noun they modify, *not* with the possessor.

Forms French possessive adjectives have the following forms.

		MASCULINE	FEMININE	PLURAL	ENGLISH EQUIVALENT
SINGULAR	FIRST PERSON	*mon*	*ma*	*mes*	my
	SECOND PERSON	*ton*	*ta*	*tes*	your
	THIRD PERSON	*son*	*sa*	*ses*	his, her, its
PLURAL	FIRST PERSON	*notre*	*notre*	*nos*	our
	SECOND PERSON	*votre*	*votre*	*vos*	your
	THIRD PERSON	*leur*	*leur*	*leurs*	their

This is quite different from English. *Son cahier* can mean either "his notebook" or "her notebook." The masculine form *son* is used, because *cahier* is masculine. For instance, Anne can say the following.

> Voici **mon** cahier, **ma** traduction et **mes** exercices.

The possessive adjectives do not indicate Anne's gender, but they do indicate the genders and numbers of the three items that she possesses.

Feminine singular nouns beginning with a vowel or silent *h* take *mon, ton, son* for their possessive adjectives.

> **mon** ami
> **mon** amie

Mon is used in both cases because *amie* begins with a vowel. Notice that these two phrases sound the same and, when spoken, do not reveal the gender of the friend.

Interrogative adjectives

Forms In French, the interrogative adjective is inflected for gender and number. It agrees with the noun it modifies.

	MASCULINE	FEMININE
SINGULAR	*quel*	*quelle*
PLURAL	*quels*	*quelles*

As long as these adjectives appear directly before the noun, they present little difficulty for the learner of French. When they are separated by the verb, however, it is harder for speakers of English to recognize them as adjectives.

Uses Interrogative adjectives are used

1. to ask a question.

> **Quel** est le devoir pour aujourd'hui?
> **Quel** cours avez-vous à 10 heures?

Whose does not exist as an interrogative adjective in French; it requires a different construction.

2. in an exclamation.

> **Quelle** jolie maison!
> **Quel** travail!

 ## Indefinite adjectives

Definition Indefinite adjectives refer to nouns or pronouns that are not defined more specifically.

> *Some students learn fast.*
> *Any girl will tell you.*
> *Both lectures are at 10 o'clock.*
> *Each/Every class has its value.*
> *I want another pen.*
> *Such behavior is terrible.*

Forms These adjectives are invariable, that is, they do not change their form. Some, however, may be used only with singular nouns (for example, *each, every, another*), some only with plural nouns (for example, *both, other*), and some with either singular or plural nouns (for example, *some*: *some coffee, some people*).

Other limiting adjectives

Ordinal numbers

These numbers indicate the order in which things come. *One, two,* and *three* (and all numbers ending in *one, two,* and *three*, except *eleven, twelve,* and *thirteen*) have irregular ordinals.

> *first, second, third*

All other ordinal numbers are formed by adding *-th*.

> *fourth, ninth, sixteenth*

Determiners

Determiners are often classified as adjectives (see page 16).

Other adjectival forms

Many other kinds of words—even though they are not adjectives themselves—may be used as adjectives (that is, to describe a noun or pronoun).

NOUN	a **philosophy** professor
PRESENT PARTICIPLE	**running** water
PAST PARTICIPLE	the **required** reading
PREPOSITIONAL PHRASE	the poster **on the wall**
RELATIVE CLAUSE	the poster **that I bought**
INFINITIVE	I wondered what **to do**.
ADVERBIAL PHRASE	People **from all around** love him.

French Indefinite adjectives

Definition French indefinite adjectives are similar to those in English.

> ***Quelques*** *étudiants apprennent vite.*
> ***N'importe quelle*** *fille vous le dira.*
> ***Les deux*** *conférences sont à 10 heures.*
> ***Chaque*** *cours a ses mérites.*
> *Je voudrais un **autre** stylo.*
> *De **telle** conduite est répréhensible.*

Forms An indefinite adjective agrees with its noun in gender and number, just as descriptive adjectives do.

French Other limiting adjectives

Ordinal numbers

Ordinal numbers are fairly easy in French. For most, *-ième* is simply added to the number.

1. *Premier/première* is irregular.

2. A few other ordinal numbers have slight spelling adjustments.

   a. If a number ends in *-e,* the *-e* is omitted.

   quatre → **quatrième**

   b. If a number ends in *-f,* the *-f* changes to *-v.*

   neuf → **neuvième**

   c. If a number ends in *-q,* the *-q* changes to *-qu.*

   cinq → **cinquième**

3. The ending *-ième* is often abbreviated as a superscript *e* (for example, 5e).

Determiners

See page 17.

French Other adjectival forms

NOUN PHRASE	*un professeur **de philosophie***
PRESENT PARTICIPLE	*l'eau **courante***
PAST PARTICIPLE	*la lecture **requise***
PREPOSITIONAL PHRASE	*l'affiche **au mur***
RELATIVE CLAUSE	*l'affiche **que j'ai achetée***
INFINITIVE	*Je me suis demandé que **faire**.*
ADVERBIAL PHRASE	*Des gens **de partout** l'aiment.*

6

Adverbs

Definition See page 7.

Forms Most English adverbs formed from descriptive adjectives add -*ly* to the adjective.

> *active ~ actively*
> *slow ~ slowly*

1. Like adjectives, adverbs may be inflected to show comparison.

POSITIVE	COMPARATIVE	SUPERLATIVE
actively	*more actively*	*most actively*
actively	*less actively*	*least actively*

The comparative is used to show the similarity or difference between how two people or things do something, or the degree of difference in qualifying an adjective or adverb. The superlative compares more than two people or things. There must also be a word to link the two points of comparison.

POSITIVE	*I walk **slowly**.*
COMPARATIVE	*John walks **more slowly than** I do.*
SUPERLATIVE	*Monica walks **the most slowly of** all.*

2. Like adjectives, some adverbs not ending in -*ly* may take -*er* and -*est* in comparisons.

> *He runs fast, but I run **faster**.*
> *Mary runs the **fastest** of all.*

3. Some adverbs form their comparison irregularly.

POSITIVE	COMPARATIVE	SUPERLATIVE
well	*better*	*best*
badly	*worse*	*worst*

Uses English adverbs are used in the following ways.

1. Adverbs answer the questions *how, when, where,* or *how much* about a verb, an adjective, or another adverb. Sometimes, a phrase takes the place of a single adverb.

> **Yesterday** he came **here** and **very** **quickly** told the story.
> WHEN   WHERE   HOW MUCH   HOW

> **This morning** he went **there** **by car**.
> WHEN   WHERE   HOW

CONTINUED ON PAGE 58 ▶

French Introducing adverbs

Forms   Most French adverbs formed from descriptive adjectives add -*ment* to the feminine form of the adjective.

> *actif(ve)* ~ **activement**
> *lent(e)* ~ **lentement**

1. Like adjectives, adverbs may show comparison.

POSITIVE	COMPARATIVE	SUPERLATIVE
activement	*plus activement*	*le plus activement*
	aussi activement	
	moins activement	*le moins activement*

The words used to link the two elements being compared are the same as for adjectives. (See **Quick Check** on page 47.)

POSITIVE	*Je marche* **lentement**.
COMPARATIVE	*Jean marche* **plus lentement que** *moi.*
SUPERLATIVE	*Monique marche* **le plus lentement de** *tous.*

2. Some of the most common French adverbs do not end in -*ment* and must be learned as vocabulary items. They are compared, however, in the same way as -*ment* adverbs.

> *Il court* **vite**, *mais je cours* **plus vite**.
> *Marie court* **le plus vite** *de tous.*

3. Two adverbs—meaning "well" and "badly"—form their comparisons irregularly.

POSITIVE	COMPARATIVE	SUPERLATIVE
bien	*mieux*	*le mieux*
mal	*pis (plus mal)*	*le pis (le plus mal)*

These forms are easy to confuse with the adjectives *bon* ("good") and *mauvais* ("bad"). It may help to remember that *bien* and *mieux* both have an *i* as the second letter and that the two three-letter words (*mal* and *pis*) go together.

Uses   French adverbs are used in the following ways.

1. See the English uses on the opposite page.

> **Hier** *il est venu* **ici** *et a* **très   vite** *raconté l'histoire.*
> WHEN   WHERE HOW MUCH HOW

> **Ce matin** *il y est allé* **en voiture**.
> WHEN   WHERE   HOW

CONTINUED ON PAGE 59 ▶

2. **Negatives.** Some adverbs make a sentence negative. These include words like *not, nowhere,* and *never.* In standard English, two negative words in one sentence express a positive, not a negative, idea.

> *He doesn't have **no** friends, but he has **too few**.*

The first clause used alone and intended as a negative is not standard English. Not only are negative adverbs included here, but negative nouns and adjectives as well.

CONTINUED ON PAGE 60 ▶

2. **Negatives**. Negatives can cause difficulties in learning French for two reasons: They have two parts, and more than one can be used in a sentence.

   a. *Ne... pas* is the equivalent of English "not." *Ne* comes before the verb in a simple tense, and *pas* comes after the verb. In the perfect (compound) tenses, the auxiliary, which agrees with the subject in person and number, is treated like a simple-tense verb.

   *Je **n'**aime **pas** Pierre.*
   *Nous **ne** sommes **pas** encore arrivés.*

   When the verb form and its subject are joined by a hyphen, they are considered one word and cannot be separated.

   ***Ne** travaillez-vous **pas**?*
   ***N'**est-elle **pas** arrivée?*

   Both *ne* and *pas* precede an infinitive.

   *Je commence à **ne pas** comprendre.*

   b. More specific negative adverbs may replace *pas*.

ne... jamais	never
ne... plus	no longer
ne... point	not at all

   *Je **n'**aime **point** Pierre.*
   ***Ne** travaillez-vous **jamais**?*

   French uses similar constructions to contrast nouns, pronouns, adjectives, and adverbs, and to contrast verbs.

   | ne... ni... ni | neither ... nor |
   | ne... ni... ne | neither ... nor |

   | *Je **ne** vois **ni** Jean **ni** Pierre.* | I see neither John nor Peter. |
   | *Il **ne** lit **ni ne** comprend le chinois.* | He neither reads nor understands Chinese. |

   In the *ne... ni* construction, *ne* comes before verbs (as with *ne... pas)* and *ni* before other parts of speech.

   Personne ("no one") and *rien* ("nothing," "anything") are negative words, but they are pronouns, not adverbs, so they are placed in the subject or object position in a sentence. *Ne* is placed before the verb, and *pas* is not used.

   | ***Personne ne** fait **rien**!* | No one is doing anything! |
   | *Je **n'**ai vu **personne**.* | I saw no one. |

   c. You can accumulate several negatives in a French sentence—which you can't do in standard English.

   | *Non! Je **ne** dis **plus jamais rien à personne**!* | No! I never tell anyone anything anymore. |

   With compound verbs, *rien* comes in the adverbial position.

   | *Je **n'**ai **rien** vu.* | I didn't see anything. |

   d. *Ne... que* ("only") is not negative, although it has a negative form. *Que* is placed before the word it modifies.

   | *Je **n'**ai **qu'**un frère.* | I have only one brother. |
   | *Je **ne** l'ai appris **qu'**aujourd'hui.* | I found out only today. |

CONTINUED ON PAGE 61 ▶

3. **Questions**. Another group of adverbs introduces questions: *when? where? how?* and *why?* The majority of adverbs answer these questions with respect to the verb, but the interrogative words themselves are adverbs too.

> **When** *does he arrive?*
> **How** *do you know that?*

4. **Relative clauses**. The same adverbs that ask questions may also be used to form relative clauses. These clauses tell when, where, how, or why the verb's action takes place and can be used in the same way.

> *We are going to the movies* **when** *we finish our work.*

Adjectives vs. adverbs

To choose the correct word, it is essential to ask yourself the following questions.

1. Am I *describing someone/something?* → adjective

2. Am I *describing how/when/where/why something is done?* → adverb

> *The* **poem** *is* **good***, and the poet* **reads** *it* **well***.*
> NOUN ADJECTIVE VERB ADVERB

> *The* **play** *is* **bad***, and it's* **badly** **performed***.*
> NOUN ADJECTIVE ADVERB VERB

This is especially important for verbs of mental or emotional state and for sensory verbs, which can be followed by either an adjective or an adverb. One of the most common examples is the following.

> *I feel* **bad***.* (= I am sick/unhappy/etc.)
> *I feel* **badly***.* (= My hands are not sensitive.)

3. **Questions**

> *Quand arrive-t-il?*
> *Comment savez-vous cela?*

4. **Relative clauses**

> *Nous allons au cinéma quand nous terminerons notre travail.*

Adjectives vs. adverbs

Le poème est bon, et le poète le lit bien.
   NOUN   ADJECTIVE   VERB ADVERB

Le pièce est mauvaise, et on la joue mal.
   NOUN   ADJECTIVE   VERB ADVERB

7

Conjunctions

English Introducing conjunctions

Definition See page 7.

Forms Conjunctions are function words; they are invariable.

Types All conjunctions are linking words, but the linked elements and their relationship with each other determine which of the three principal types a conjunction belongs to: coordinating, subordinating, or adverbial.

Uses English conjunctions are used as follows.

1. A **coordinating conjunction** links two equal elements that have the same grammatical construction. The two elements may be single words, phrases, or entire clauses.

NOUNS	*John **and** Mary*
INFINITIVES	*to be **or** not to be*
INDEPENDENT CLAUSES	*We came, **but** he was not there.*

   Correlatives, which occur in pairs, are a subgroup of coordinating conjunctions.

   ***Both** John **and** Mary are in the class.*

2. A **subordinating conjunction** joins unequal elements. One element is subordinated to the other. The conjunction introduces the subordinate clause (the one that cannot stand alone as a sentence).

CONTRAST	***Although** he is hurrying, he is late.*
TIME	*We speak French **when** the Duponts are here.*
CAUSE	***Because** this course is easy, we all get "A"s.*

   Notice that the main idea of the sentence is in the main (independent) clause. The subordinate clause tells about the time, way, cause, or conditions involved and may show a contrast. Notice also that the main clause need not come first. You could reverse the order of the clauses in each example above without changing the meaning of the sentence.

   There is also a subgroup of correlative subordinating conjunctions (for example, *if . . . then* and *so . . . that*).

   *That course is **so** hard **that** many students fail.*

3. An **adverbial conjunction** is sometimes called a "conjunctive adverb." Grammarians are not sure whether they are really adverbs or conjunctions. Words and phrases like *therefore, perhaps, also, for example, as a result,* and *in other words* fall into this category.

French Introducing conjunctions

Uses   French conjunctions are used as follows.

1. Coordinating conjunctions

NOUNS   *Jean **et** Marie*

INFINITIVES   *être **ou** ne pas être*

INDEPENDENT CLAUSES   *Nous sommes venus, **mais** il n'était pas là.*

Correlative conjunctions are a subgroup of coordinating conjunctions.

***Et** Jean **et** Marie sont dans la classe.*

2. Subordinating conjunctions

CONTRAST   ***Bien qu'**il se dépêche, il est en retard.*

TIME   *Nous parlons français **quand** les Dupont sont ici.*

CAUSE   ***Parce que** ce cours est facile, nous avons tous des "A."*

Correlative conjunctions are a subgroup of subordinating conjunctions.

*Ce cours est **si** difficile **que** beaucoup d'étudiants échouent.*

3. Adverbial conjunctions

donc, peut-être, par exemple, etc.

Interjections

Definition   See page 7.

Forms   Interjections are normally invariable exclamations.

Uses   As an exclamation, an interjection is often merely a sound meant to convey emotion (for example, *ow!*). It has no grammatical connection with the other words in the sentence and is set off by commas.

French: Introducing interjections

Interjections present no problems for the learner of French; they are simply vocabulary items. Following are some common ones.

Aïe!
Heu!
Hein!
Hélas!

9

Prepositions

Prepositions in any language are very tricky words. Most of them have basic meanings, but when they are used in phrasal verb constructions, that meaning can change. A phrasal verb is a combination of a verb plus (usually) a preposition that has a meaning different from the combined meanings of the words. You may think, for example, that you know what *up* means, but consider the following sentence.

> First he cut the tree **down**, then he cut it **up**.

People learning English would be confused by that sentence, and it is not an isolated example. Take the case of a friend telephoning John's house early in the morning and asking for him. John's wife might reply as follows.

> He'll be **down** as soon as he's **up**.

In other words, after learning a preposition and its basic meanings, one must be alert to how it is used in phrasal verb constructions. Often, the meanings of a single preposition will spread over several pages of a dictionary.

Definition   See page 7.

Forms   A preposition is a function word; it is invariable. It can be a single word or a group of words (for example, *by* and *in spite of*).

Uses   A preposition links a noun or pronoun (its object) to other words in the sentence and shows the object's relationship to them. In formal English, a preposition is followed immediately by its object.

> **to** the store
> **about** the subject

In informal English, a preposition is often placed at the end of the clause or sentence, especially in questions and relative clauses.

> **What** is she waiting **for**?
>   INSTEAD OF **For what** is she waiting?
> This is the one **that** he is referring **to**.
>   INSTEAD OF This is the one **to which** he is referring.

French Introducing prepositions

Forms A French preposition can be one or several words; examples are *par* ("by") and *à côté de* ("beside").

Prepositions are invariable, except for *à* and *de,* which combine with the definite articles *le* and *les.*

	SINGULAR	PLURAL
MASCULINE	*à + le → au*	*à + les → aux*
	de + le → du	*de + les → des*
FEMININE	*à + la → à la*	*à + les → aux*
	de + la → de la	*de + les → des*

This contraction takes place even if *à* or *de* or the definite article is part of a longer word or expression.

> *à côté de + le restaurant → à côté du restaurant*
> *près de + lequel → près duquel*

Never expect a one-to-one equivalence between English and French prepositions. They are capricious in both languages.

Uses In English, a preposition comes before its object in formal speech and writing. In French (and many other languages), it must *nearly always* do so. Prepositions are not placed at the end of a clause or sentence except in the most informal speech.

Special problems with prepositions

1. Geographical names require specific prepositions to express "to" and "from."

	FEMININE		MASCULINE	
	"to"	*"from"*	*"to"*	*"from"*
COUNTRIES	*en*	*de*	*à* + definite article	*de* + definite article
CONTINENTS	*en*	*de*	—	—
STATES* AND PROVINCES	*en*	*de*	*dans* + definite article	*de* + definite article
CITIES†	*à*	*de*	*à*	*de*

CONTINUED ON PAGE 74 ▶

---

* The states of the United States are masculine except for a few, well-known ones ending in *-e*: *la Californie, la Floride, la Pennsylvanie, la Caroline du Nord,* etc.

† If the name of the city contains a definite article, the article remains.
   au Caire
   à la Nouvelle-Orléans

2. Verbs are often followed by infinitives. If two verbs are used to express a single thought, the *first* determines whether a preposition (and which one) is used to introduce the infinitive that follows. There can even be more than two infinitives in a string (see the example below). In every case, if a verb is followed by an infinitive, the first of the two determines the preposition.

Following is a list of verbs and the prepositions they take when followed by an infinitive. Some of these verbs take a direct or indirect object before the preposition.

à	*de*	NONE
aider	choisir	aimer
apprendre	décider	aller
avoir	demander	croire
chercher	dire	devoir
commencer (usually)	écrire	écouter
continuer	essayer	entendre
encourager	finir	faire
inviter	oublier	falloir
jouer	permettre	laisser
penser	refuser	oser
réussir	regretter	pouvoir
s'intéresser	suggérer	préférer
se décider	venir (de)	regarder
se mettre		savoir
		sembler
		valoir
		voir
		vouloir

Aller requires no preposition before an infinitive.

    Je **vais** lire ce livre.   I am going to read this book.

Commencer takes *à* before an infinitive.

    Je **commence à** lire davantage.   I am beginning to read more.

Essayer takes *de* before an infinitive.

    J'essaie de commencer mon devoir.   I am trying to start my assignment.
    Je vais essayer de commencer à lire   I am going to try to begin to read
       ce livre.   this book.

In each of these cases, it is the first of a group of two verbs that determines which preposition, if any, is to be used before the second.

Verbs formed with prefixes usually require the same preposition as the basic verb.

    Je recommence **à** le faire.
    Je promets **de** le faire.

10

Verbs

Introducing verbs

Definition See page 7.

Forms English has fewer inflected verb forms than any continental European language. Many English verbs have only four forms (for example, *talk, talks, talked, talking*); some have five forms (for example, *sing, sings, sang, sung, singing*).

In some systems of grammar, it is said that, technically, English has only two tenses—present and past—and that other temporal concepts are expressed by periphrastic verbal constructions. This means that English uses helping verbs and other expressions to convey temporal differences. Verbs are presented here in a more traditional way, because it will help you see the parallels between English and French constructions. Following are the principal parts of an English verb.

INFINITIVE	SIMPLE PAST	PAST PARTICIPLE	PRESENT PARTICIPLE
talk	*talked*	*talked*	*talking*
sing	*sang*	*sung*	*singing*

Some words used to identify verb forms are **conjugation**, **tense**, **voice**, **transitive**, **intransitive**, and **mood**.

Conjugation

This word has two meanings.

1. In Latin and in modern Romance languages, verbs are classified into groups, or conjugations, by their infinitive endings. English and German have only *regular* and *irregular* (sometimes called *weak* and *strong*) verbs. Weak verbs take a regular ending to form the past (for example, *talk ~ talked* and *follow ~ followed*). Strong verbs often change the vowel in their past forms and may look completely different from the infinitive (for example, *sing ~ sang* and *go ~ went*).

2. Conjugation also refers to a list, by person, of each form in a given tense. Latin has six forms in each tense. Following are the present-tense forms of *amare* ("to love").

	SINGULAR	PLURAL
FIRST PERSON	*amo* I love	*amamus* we love
SECOND PERSON	*amas* you (singular) love	*amatis* you (plural) love
THIRD PERSON	*amat* he/she loves	*amant* they love

Since each form is different, it is not necessary to use a pronoun subject: The verb ending tells you who the subject is. The same is true for Spanish and Italian today.

In English, verbs can be conjugated but usually are not, because there is only one inflected ending: *-s* is added to the third-person singular of the simple present tense.

	SINGULAR	PLURAL
FIRST PERSON	*I speak*	*we speak*
SECOND PERSON	*you speak*	*you speak*
THIRD PERSON	*he/she speaks*	*they speak*

The pronoun (or a noun) is required with every verb form, because otherwise it would not be known who or what the subject is.

Tense

This word comes from Latin *tempus* via French *temps,* meaning "time." The tense tells *when* something happened, *how long* it lasted, and whether it is *completed.*

Voice

English has two voices: active and passive. **Active voice** means that the subject is or is doing something.

> *Mary is happy.*
> *Mary reads the newspaper.*

In these examples, *Mary* is the subject.

Passive voice means that the subject is acted on by an agent. The verb tells what happens to the subject.

> *The newspaper is read by Mary.*

In this example, *newspaper* is the subject.

Transitive verbs

These verbs require an object to express a complete meaning.

> *Mr. White surprised a burglar.*

In this example, the verb *surprised* is transitive, because it takes an object, *burglar.* If we omitted the object, the sentence would not make sense; it would be incomplete.

Intransitive verbs

These verbs do not require an object.

> *Paul sat down.*

Here, the verb *sat* is intransitive, because it has no object; *down* is an adverb.

English has many verbs that can be either transitive or intransitive.

Peter	***eats***	*dinner*	*at 7 o'clock.*
The butcher	***weighs***	*the meat.*	
SUBJECT	TRANSITIVE VERB	DIRECT OBJECT	

Peter	***eats***	*at 7 o'clock.*
The butcher	***weighs***	*a lot.*
SUBJECT	INTRANSITIVE VERB	

Mood

This grammatical concept indicates the mood, or attitude, of the speaker. Is the speaker stating a fact? Offering a possibility that has not happened yet? Making a recommendation? Giving an order? Three moods are used to express these ideas: indicative, imperative, and subjunctive. The indicative is by far the most common mood. The other two are used in special circumstances and are discussed below.

English Introducing questions

Forms   There are four ways to ask a question in English.

1. Place a question mark after a statement and raise the pitch of your voice at the end of the statement when saying it aloud.

   Anne is here already?
   That's Mark's idea?

2. Add a "tag," repeating the verb or auxiliary verb as a negative question. In English, the specific tag depends on the subject and the verb.

   *Peter is happy, **isn't he**?*
   *They came on time, **didn't they**?*

3. Invert the subject and an auxiliary or modal verb or the verb *to be*.

PRESENT	***Do you** have any brothers?*
PRESENT PROGRESSIVE	***Is Peter** buying his books?*
PRESENT	***Does Peter** buy his books?*
PRESENT PERFECT	***Has Peter** bought his books?*
PRESENT	***May I** see you this evening?*
PRESENT	***Is Robert** here today?*

4. Use an interrogative word.

   ***Where** is the library?*
   ***When** does the library open?*

French · Introducing questions

Forms There are five ways to ask a question in French.

1. Place a question mark after a statement and raise the pitch of your voice at the end of the statement when saying it aloud. This method is usually limited to conversations (oral and written).

   > *Anne est déjà ici?*
   > *C'est l'idée de Marc?*

2. Place *n'est-ce pas* after a statement with which you expect the hearer or reader to agree.

   > *Pierre est content, **n'est-ce pas**?*

3. Invert the pronoun subject and verb. You do not need an auxiliary verb to form a question, as you do in English.

   > ***Avez-vous** des frères?*

   Do not use inversion with *je*. In the third-person singular of *-er* verbs, add *-t-* to make pronunciation easier.

   > *parlez-vous* BUT *parle-**t**-il, parle-**t**-elle, parle-**t**-on*

   If the subject is a noun, do not invert it with the verb. For example, to make a question of the statement *Pierre achète ses livres,*

   a. state the noun first: *Pierre…*

   b. invert the verb and the personal pronoun for *Pierre* (*il*): *Pierre achète-t-il…*

   c. complete the sentence: *Pierre achète-t-il ses livres?*

4. Place *est-ce que* at the beginning of the statement.

   > ***Est-ce que** la bibliothéque est ouverte?*

5. Use an interrogative word, with or without verb-pronoun inversion and with or without *est-ce que.*

   > ***Où** est la bibliothéque?*
   > ***Quand** la bibliothèque **est-elle** ouverte?*
   > ***Quand est-ce que** la bibliothèque est ouverte?*

These rules apply to a simple tense (one in which the verb is expressed by one word). In compound tenses (those that use two or more words to form the verb), the auxiliary verb is treated in the same way as in simple tenses.

> ***Avez-vous** parlé?*
> *Pierre **a-t-il** acheté ses livres?*

Word order

WITH NEGATIVES The verb-pronoun group is joined by a hyphen. A hyphenated group may never be broken up. Thus, *ne… pas* (or any other negative form) is placed around the whole group.

> *Pierre **n'a-t-il pas** acheté ses livres?*

WITH PRONOUN OBJECTS As with statements, pronoun objects go directly before the verb in questions.

> ***Les** avez-vous?*
> ***Vous** a-t-il vu?*
> *Ne **m'**avez-vous pas vu?*

WITH OTHER KINDS OF QUESTIONS When you use intonation, *n'est-ce pas*, or *est-ce que* to ask a question, the word order is the same as for a statement. See the examples above.

Introducing verbals

Definition   Verbals are forms of the verb that are not finite, that is, do not agree with a subject and do not function as the predicate of a sentence. There are five types of verbals: present infinitive, past infinitive, gerund, present participle (also called the gerundive), and past participle.

 Present infinitives

Definition   The present infinitive is the basic form of the verb, as it appears in a dictionary.

Forms   The infinitive is often identified by the word *to* preceding it. However, *to* is omitted in many infinitive constructions, especially after verbs like *can* and *let*. Compare the following sentences, both of which contain the infinitive *swim*.

> *I know how **to swim**.*
> *I can **swim**.*

Uses   In addition to completing the verb, as in the above examples, an infinitive may serve as the subject or object of a sentence, as an adjective, or as an adverb.

SUBJECT	***To err*** *is human.*
OBJECT	*He hopes **to come** soon.*
ADJECTIVE	*English is the subject **to study**.*
ADVERB	***To tell the truth**, he wants it more than ever.*

Infinitives may also have their own direct objects and other modifiers.

> *I am able **to do** that   easily.*
>   DIRECT OBJECT   ADVERB

English Past infinitives

Forms   The past infinitive is formed with the present infinitive of the auxiliary verb plus the past participle of the main verb.

> *to go* (present infinitive) → *to have gone* (past infinitive)

Uses   The past infinitive is used in the same ways as the present infinitive.

> ***To have quit*** *is terrible.*

French Present infinitives

Forms   French verbs are grouped in three conjugations by the ending of their infinitives: *-er* (the most common), *-ir,* and *-re.*

Uses   The French infinitive may be used in several ways.

SUBJECT/COMPLEMENT	***Voir,** c'est **croire.***
OBJECT	*Il souhaite **arriver** bientôt.*
ADJECTIVE	*L'anglais, c'est le sujet à **étudier.***
ADVERB	***À vrai dire,** il le veut plus que jamais.*
OBJECT OF A PREPOSITION	*Pour bien **faire,** travaillez sérieusement.*

The prepositions *en* and *après* do not take a present infinitive (see below).

Infinitives may have objects (either nouns or pronouns) and be negated or otherwise modified.

DIRECT OBJECT/INDIRECT OBJECT	*Je veux **vous le** montrer.*
NEGATIVE/ADVERB	*Je préfère **ne pas** venir **trop tôt.***

The negative *ne pas* precedes the infinitive.

French Past infinitives

Forms   Past infinitives are formed as in English, with the present infinitive of the auxiliary (*avoir* or *être,* depending on the verb) plus the past participle.

> *parler* (present infinitive) → *avoir parlé* (past infinitive)
> *aller* (present infinitive) → *être allé* (past infinitive)

The past infinitive must be used with the preposition *après.*

> ***Après avoir mangé**, il est parti.*   After eating (having eaten), he left.
> OR After he ate, he left.

English Gerunds

Definition   Gerunds are often called verbal nouns.

Forms   The English gerund is formed by adding *-ing* to the infinitive form of the verb.

> *sing* → *singing*
> *run* → *running*
> *bite* → *biting*

Uses   Gerunds have the same functions as other nouns (see page 10).

> SUBJECT   ***Walking*** *is good for you.*
> OBJECT   *I like **singing**.*

Gerunds may also have objects and modifiers.

> ***Making*** *money   quickly is many people's goal.*
> DIRECT OBJECT   ADVERB

English Participles

Definition   Participles are verbal adjectives that constitute the third and fourth principal parts of a verb.

Forms   English has two participles.

1. **Present participles** (the fourth principal part) end in *-ing*.

   singing
   talking
   managing

2. **Past participles** (the third principal part) end in *-ed* or *-n* for regular verbs.

   tried
   gathered
   concentrated
   given

   To determine the past participle of an irregular verb, say, "Today I go; yesterday I went; I have gone; I am going." The form used after "I have" is the past participle. In the dictionary, the principal parts are given for every irregular verb.

CONTINUED ON PAGE 84 ▶

French Gerunds

French has no gerund; the infinitive is used as the verbal noun (see the first example above under present infinitives). Infinitives may be modified.

> *Gagner **vite** de l'argent, c'est le but de bien des gens.*

French Participles

Forms   French has two participles.

1. **Present participles** end in *-ant*. This ending is added to the first-person plural of the present tense after dropping the ending *-ons*.

   > *nous parlons* → ***parlant***
   > *nous finissons* → ***finissant***
   > *nous dormons* → ***dormant***
   > *nous rendons* → ***rendant***

   Three French verbs have irregular present participles.

   > *être* → ***étant***
   > *avoir* → ***ayant***
   > *savoir* → ***sachant***

   In order for all forms to keep the same consonant sounds as the infinitive, verbs ending in *-cer* and *-ger* make a slight, but regular, change to form the present participle: *-Cer* verbs put a cedilla under the *-c-*, and *-ger* verbs add *-e* before endings that begin with *a* or *o*.

   > *commençons* → ***commençant***
   > *mangeons* → ***mangeant***

2. **Past participles** have different endings for the different conjugations. For regular verbs, the infinitive ending *-er, -ir, -re,* or *-oir* is dropped, and *-e, -i,* or *-u* is added.

   > *parler* → ***parlé***
   > *finir* → ***fini***
   > *rendre* → ***rendu***
   > *falloir* → ***fallu***

CONTINUED ON PAGE 85 ▶

Uses The two types of participles have the same basic uses.

1. As part of a compound verb (one consisting of two or more words)

PRESENT PROGRESSIVE	*He **is talking**.*
PAST PERFECT	*They **have given**.*

2. As an adjective

   a ***talking*** doll
   a ***proven*** fact

3. In an absolute phrase modifying a noun

   Walking *along the street, he met Robin.*
   Seen *from the front, the building was even more imposing.*

In the two examples above, *he* is *walking* and *the building* was *seen*.

A number of French verbs have irregular past participles; following are some of the most common.*

avoir → eu	dire → dit	mettre → mis	être → été	faire → fait
boire → bu	écrire → écrit	prendre → pris	naître → né	mourir → mort
croire → cru				venir → venu
devoir → dû				
lire → lu				
pouvoir → pu				
recevoir → reçu				
savoir → su				
voir → vu				
vouloir → voulu				

Uses   A **present participle** is used

1. after the preposition *en* to express "while doing something."

   En rentrant, *j'ai vu Paul.*

   All other prepositions are followed by an infinitive.

2. as an adjective. (Adjectives ending in *-ant* were once verbals.)

   un roseau **pensant**   a thinking reed (Blaise Pascal)

3. as an absolute modifying a noun or pronoun.

   Sachant *qu'il est difficile, j'évite M. Jones.*

A **past participle** is used

1. as a noun.

   le premier **venu**   just anybody (literally, the first one who came)

2. as an adjective.

   un fait **prouvé**

3. as the second element of a compound verb form.

   j'ai **parlé**
   il aura **fini**

4. in an absolute phrase modifying a noun or pronoun.

   Vu *de face, le bâtiment était même plus imposant.*

---

*When a prefix is added to any of these verbs, the past participle shows the same irregularities: *mettre, remettre, promettre* → **mis, remis, promis**.

Indicative mood

The verbs on pages 86–107 are all in the indicative mood. It is the one used for stating facts and for making assertions as though they were facts.

English Present tenses

Definition   The present tense is defined by its uses (see below).

Forms   There are three present tenses in English: simple present, present progressive, and present emphatic.

1. **Simple present.** There is only one inflected form in the simple present: the third-person singular, which adds *-s* to the basic verb form.

	SINGULAR	PLURAL
FIRST PERSON	*I sing*	*we sing*
SECOND PERSON	*you sing*	*you sing*
THIRD PERSON	*he/she sings*	*they sing*

2. **Present progressive.** This tense is formed with the present tense of *to be* plus the present participle.

	SINGULAR	PLURAL
FIRST PERSON	*I am singing*	*we are singing*
SECOND PERSON	*you are singing*	*you are singing*
THIRD PERSON	*he/she is singing*	*they are singing*

3. **Present emphatic.** This tense is formed with the present tense of *to do* plus the infinitive.

	SINGULAR	PLURAL
FIRST PERSON	*I do sing*	*we do sing*
SECOND PERSON	*you do sing*	*you do sing*
THIRD PERSON	*he/she does sing*	*they do sing*

CONTINUED ON PAGE 88 ▶

French Present tense

Forms   The French present tense is easier than English because there is only one tense, not three. It is more difficult, however, because each conjugation has different endings and because French has many more irregular verbs. One system of classifying irregular French verbs by their conjugation patterns may be found in Appendix C.

1. *-er* **verbs**. Drop the infinitive ending (*-er*) and add *-e, -es, -e; -ons, -ez, -ent*.

	SINGULAR	PLURAL
FIRST PERSON	*je parle*	*nous parlons*
SECOND PERSON	*tu parles*	*vous parlez*
THIRD PERSON	*il/elle/on parle*	*ils/elles parlent*

2. *-ir* **verbs** (**finir** type). Drop the infinitive ending (*-ir*) and add *-is, -is, -it; -issons, -issez, -issent*.

	SINGULAR	PLURAL
FIRST PERSON	*je finis*	*nous finissons*
SECOND PERSON	*tu finis*	*vous finissez*
THIRD PERSON	*il/elle finit*	*ils/elles finissent*

This pattern is used for all *-ir* verbs except those listed under *dormir* (below) and some irregular verbs (see Appendix C).

-ir **verbs** (**dormir** type). Drop the *-ir* ending and the final consonant (in the singular forms) of the infinitive and add *-s, -s, -t; -ons, -ez, -ent*.

	SINGULAR	PLURAL
FIRST PERSON	*je dors*	*nous dormons*
SECOND PERSON	*tu dors*	*vous dormez*
THIRD PERSON	*il/elle dort*	*ils/elles dorment*

Verbs like *dormir* include *partir, sortir, servir, mentir, courir,* and their compounds.

3. *-re* **verbs**. Drop the infinitive ending (*-re*) and add *-s, -s, —; -ons, -ez, -ent*.

	SINGULAR	PLURAL
FIRST PERSON	*je rends*	*nous rendons*
SECOND PERSON	*tu rends*	*vous rendez*
THIRD PERSON	*il/elle rend*	*ils/elles rendent*

CONTINUED ON PAGE 89 ▶

Uses   The **simple present** is used for

1. an action or state occurring in the present.

   They **speak** *Chinese.*

2. an habitual action that is still true.

   I always **study** *in the evening.*

3. existing facts and eternal truths.

   Paris **is** *the capital of France.*
   I **think***, therefore I* **am***.* (René Descartes)

The **present progressive** is used to

1. stress the continuing nature of the verb's action in either a statement or a question.

   I **am** *still* **trying***!*
   Are *you* **going** *to the library now?*

2. make a future action seem more immediate.

   We **are reading** *this book next week.*
   I **am going** *to the show tomorrow.*

The **present emphatic** is used to

1. add emphasis or contradict.

   I **do want** *to do well.*
   They **do** *not* **do** *that!*

2. form questions or negative statements.

   Do *you* **go** *to the lake in the summer?*
   I **do** *not* **know** *what you are talking about.*

Uses

1. All of the uses listed for the three present tenses in English are filled by this one tense in French. To emphasize that one is in the act of doing something, use the idiom *être en train de* + infinitive.

> *Je ne veux pas sortir maintenant; je **suis en train de préparer** notre dîner.*

> I don't want to go out now; I'm in the middle of fixing our dinner.

2. French uses the present tense with *depuis* to express an action begun in the past that is still going on in the present.

> *J'**attends** la lettre **depuis** dix jours.*

> I have been waiting for the letter for 10 days. (I began waiting 10 days ago, and I am still waiting.)

English Past tenses

Definition The past tenses describe actions or states in the past.

Forms There are three past tenses, each corresponding to one of the three present tenses discussed in the previous section. (For perfect tenses, see pages 96–105.)

1. The **simple past** is the second principal part of the verb (see page 76). It is not inflected; all of the forms are the same. The simple past of weak verbs ends in *-ed* (for example, *talked* and *wished*). Strong verbs have irregular past forms.

	SINGULAR	PLURAL
FIRST PERSON	*I sang*	*we sang*
SECOND PERSON	*you sang*	*you sang*
THIRD PERSON	*he/she sang*	*they sang*

2. The **past progressive** is formed with the simple past of the verb *to be* plus the present participle of the main verb.

	SINGULAR	PLURAL
FIRST PERSON	*I was singing*	*we were singing*
SECOND PERSON	*you were singing*	*you were singing*
THIRD PERSON	*he/she was singing*	*they were singing*

3. The **past emphatic** is formed with the simple past of the verb *to do* plus the infinitive.

	SINGULAR	PLURAL
FIRST PERSON	*I did sing*	*we did sing*
SECOND PERSON	*you did sing*	*you did sing*
THIRD PERSON	*he/she did sing*	*they did sing*

Uses The three past tenses closely parallel the three present tenses in usage, except that the action takes place in the past. The simple past is a statement of a fact, the past progressive emphasizes the duration or continuation of an action at a given moment in the past, and the past emphatic stresses a statement and is used to form negatives and questions.

Other past forms

Other expressions provide special past meanings.

1. Immediate past action: *to have just* plus the past participle

   *Mary **has just arrived** this minute.*

2. Habitual past action: *used to* or *would* plus the infinitive

   *I **used to go** to the movies every week.*
   *For a long time, I **would see** them every day.*

3. Repeated past action: *kept (on)* plus the present participle

   *He **kept (on) doing** it.*

Forms The imperfect tense is formed with the verb stem plus special endings. The stem is formed by dropping the *-ons* from the first-person plural of the present tense.

parler (nous parl-)	finir (nous finiss-)	dormir (nous dorm-)	rendre (nous rend-)
je parlais	je finissais	je dormais	je rendais
tu parlais	tu finissais	tu dormais	tu rendais
il/elle parlait	il/elle finissait	il/elle dormait	il/elle rendait
nous parlions	nous finissions	nous dormions	nous rendions
vous parliez	vous finissiez	vous dormiez	vous rendiez
ils/elles parlaient	ils/elles finissaient	ils/elles dormaient	ils/elles rendaient

Être is the only French verb that is irregular in the imperfect. The stem is *ét-*, but the endings are regular (*j'étais, nous étions*, etc.). Some verbs that have only third-person singular subjects are based on a "projected" form for *nous*; for example, the imperfect of *falloir* (*nous fallons*) is *il fallait*.

Uses The French imperfect tense is used for

1. description: What you are describing is more important than the action.

2. habitual action: See the English "used to/would" construction.

3. duration, or continuing action: See the English past progressive.

4. repeated action: See the English "kept (on)" construction.

The imperfect tense is used on the basis of these principles, not on a one-to-one correspondence with English tenses or idioms. The imperfect is used many times when the simple past tense is used in English.

DESCRIPTION	*C'**était** lundi et il **pleuvait**.*	It was Monday, and it was raining.
HABITUAL ACTION/ DESCRIPTION	*J'**allais** à l'école quand j'**étais** enfant.*	I went to school when I was a child.
DURATION	*Il **lisait** toute la soireé.*	He read all evening.

Other past tenses

Other tenses used to describe past time are the passé composé (see page 97); the pluperfect (see page 101); the passé simple and passé antérieur (see page 168); and the past subjunctive (see pages 111 and 169).

PASSÉ COMPOSÉ VS. IMPARFAIT

PASSÉ COMPOSÉ	IMPARFAIT
Event happened once	Event happened often (repeated/habitual)
Finished and completed event	Continuing, unfinished event
Series of distinct events	Description
*Elle **a fini** ses devoirs.*	*Elle **finissait** souvent très tard.*
*Le téléphone **a sonné***	*pendant qu'il **dormait**.*
*Jean **est arrivé** à Paris, **a trouvé** un hôtel et y **est resté**.*	*Jean **était** un étudiant américain qui **arrivait** à Paris en juin et y **passait** ses vacances.*

Other past forms

1. For the immediate past, use *venir de* plus an infinitive.

   *Marie **vient d'**arriver.*   Mary has just arrived.

2. For "used to" or "would" plus infinitive, use the imperfect tense.

English Future tenses

Definition   Future tenses describe events that have not yet taken place.

Forms   There are only two tenses for future time: the future and the future progressive. Both are compound tenses, that is, they require more than one word to form them.

1. The **future tense** is formed by using the auxiliary verb *will* plus the infinitive of the main verb.

	SINGULAR	PLURAL
FIRST PERSON	*I will sing*	*we will sing*
SECOND PERSON	*you will sing*	*you will sing*
THIRD PERSON	*he/she will sing*	*they will sing*

2. The **future progressive tense** is formed with the future of *to be* plus the present participle. It therefore requires three words.

	SINGULAR	PLURAL
FIRST PERSON	*I will be singing*	*we will be singing*
SECOND PERSON	*you will be singing*	*you will be singing*
THIRD PERSON	*he/she will be singing*	*they will be singing*

NOTES

1. There are no irregular future tense forms in English.

2. *Will* is often contracted to *'ll*.

> *We'll do it tomorrow.*
> *You'll be studying that next week.*

Uses   The distinction between the future and future progressive tenses is the same as that between the corresponding tenses in the present tenses (see page 88). They are used

1. to express an action or state that will happen or exist in the future.

2. in Type 1 conditional sentences, where the *if*-clause is in the present. (See **Quick Check** on page 104.)

> *If you **study**, you **will succeed**.*

Other future forms

Another way to express future action is an idiomatic use of *to go* plus the infinitive of the main verb.

> *I **am going to sing** tomorrow.*

French Future tense

Forms   There is only one future tense in French. It is formed with a stem plus special endings. The stem is the full infinitive form (but not the final *e* on -*re* verbs), and the endings are -*ai*, -*as*, -*a*; -*ons*, -*ez*, -*ont*.

NOTES

1. Future stems always end in -*r*.

2. The endings are the same as those of the present tense of *avoir*, except that there is no *av*- in the first- and second-person plural.

parler	*finir*	*dormir*	*rendre* (NO FINAL *e*)	*être* (IRREGULAR)
je parlerai	*je finirai*	*je dormirai*	*je rendrai*	*je serai*
tu parleras	*tu finiras*	*tu dormiras*	*tu rendras*	*tu seras*
il/elle parlera	*il/elle finira*	*il/elle dormira*	*il/elle rendra*	*il/elle sera*
nous parlerons	*nous finirons*	*nous dormirons*	*nous rendrons*	*nous serons*
vous parlerez	*vous finirez*	*vous dormirez*	*vous rendrez*	*vous serez*
ils/elles parleront	*ils/elles finiront*	*ils/elles dormiront*	*ils/elles rendront*	*ils/elles seront*

A number of French verbs have irregular stems in the future, even though their endings are regular.

aller → *ir*-	*courir* → *courr*-	*avoir* → *aur*-	*être* → *ser*-
envoyer → *enverr*-	*tenir* → *tiendr*-	*devoir* → *devr*-	*faire* → *fer*-
	venir → *viendr*-	*falloir* → *faudr*-	
		mourir → *mourr*-	
		pleuvoir → *pleuvr*-	
		pouvoir → *pourr*-	
		recevoir → *recevr*-	
		savoir → *saur*-	
		valoir → *vaudr*-	
		voir → *verr*-	
		vouloir → *voudr*-	

-*Er* verbs that have a spelling change before a silent *e* in the present (for example, *payer* → *je paie*, *appeler* → *j'appelle*, and *acheter* → *j'achète*) make this change in the future too, since the last *e* is silent when it is part of the future stem (*je paierai*, *j'appellerai*, and *j'achèterai*).

Uses   The future tense in French is used

1. to express an action or state that will happen or exist.

2. in Type 1 conditional sentences, where the *if*-clause is in the present. (See **Quick Check** on page 105.)

> *Si vous **étudiez**, vous **réussirez**.*

3. after *quand*, *lorsque*, *dès que*, and *aussitôt que* when future time is meant.

> *Quand il **arrivera**, nous dînerons.* (He's not here yet.)
> *Je vous l'expliquerai, dès que je le **comprendrai** moi-même.* (I don't understand yet.)

Other future forms

Like *to go* plus an infinitive in English, the present tense of *aller* plus the infinitive of the main verb can express future time or intention in French.

> *Je **vais chanter** demain.*

English Conditional tenses

Definition Many grammarians do not consider the conditional to be a true tense, but rather a mood. We consider it a tense here, however, since this analysis will make its parallels with French obvious.

Forms The **conditional tense** is formed with the auxiliary verb *would* plus the infinitive of the main verb.

	SINGULAR	PLURAL
FIRST PERSON	*I would sing*	*we would sing*
SECOND PERSON	*you would sing*	*you would sing*
THIRD PERSON	*he/she would sing*	*they would sing*

The **conditional progressive tense** is formed with the conditional of the verb *to be* plus the present participle. It therefore requires three words.

	SINGULAR	PLURAL
FIRST PERSON	*I would be singing*	*we would be singing*
SECOND PERSON	*you would be singing*	*you would be singing*
THIRD PERSON	*he/she would be singing*	*they would be singing*

Would is often contracted to *'d*.

> *I'd go if you did.*

Uses The conditional is used

1. in Type 2 conditional sentences (*If* CONDITION, *(then)* RESULT.).

   *If I were rich, (then) I **would go** to Europe every year.*

2. to convey the future from a past perspective.

FUTURE	*On Sunday, John said, "OK, I **will** see you on Monday."*
CONDITIONAL	*On Tuesday, Robert says, "John said that he **would** see us on Monday."*

Conditional tense

Definition In French, the conditional is often considered a mood rather than a tense, since it expresses speculation, not facts. This distinction, however, has no practical effect on its forms or uses.

Forms The conditional tense is formed with the future stem (see page 93) and the *imparfait* endings (see page 91). All verbs follow this pattern.

parler (FUTURE *je parlerai*)	*finir* (FUTURE *je finirai*)	*dormir* (FUTURE *je dormirai*)
je parlerais	*je finirais*	*je dormirais*
tu parlerais	*tu finirais*	*tu dormirais*
il/elle parlerait	*il/elle finirait*	*il/elle dormirait*
nous parlerions	*nous finirions*	*nous dormirions*
vous parleriez	*vous finiriez*	*vous dormiriez*
ils/elles parleraient	*ils/elles finiraient*	*ils/elles dormiraient*

rendre (FUTURE *je rendrai*)	*être* (FUTURE *je serai*)
je rendrais	*je serais*
tu rendrais	*tu serais*
il/elle rendrait	*il/elle serait*
nous rendrions	*nous serions*
vous rendriez	*vous seriez*
ils/elles rendraient	*ils/elles seraient*

Since the conditional stem is the same as the future stem, the same rules apply for spelling-change verbs (see page 93): *j'appellerais, je paierais, j'achèterais,* etc.

Uses Like the English conditional, the conditional in French is used

1. in Type 2 conditional sentences (*Si* CONDITION [*imparfait*], RESULT [*conditional*].). (See **Quick Check** on page 105.)

   *Si j'**étais** riche, j'**irais** en Europe tous les ans.*

2. to convey the future from a past perspective.

   *Dimanche Jean a dit: "OK, je vous **verrai** lundi."*
   *Mardi Robert dit: "Jean a dit qu'il nous **verrait** lundi."*

 **Perfect tenses**

Definition   Perfect tenses express

1. the time of the action or state.

2. the fact that it is completed.

"Perfect" in this sense comes from Latin *perfectus,* meaning "finished" or "completed." If something has been perfected, it needs no further work. "Perfect" here, then, does not mean "ideal."

Types   There are four perfect tenses corresponding to each of the tenses already discussed: present, past, future, and conditional.

 **Present perfect tense**

Forms   The present perfect tense is formed with the present tense of the verb *to have* plus the past participle of the main verb.

	SINGULAR	PLURAL
FIRST PERSON	*I have sung*	*we have sung*
SECOND PERSON	*you have sung*	*you have sung*
THIRD PERSON	*he/she has sung*	*they have sung*

Uses   This tense indicates that from the point of view of the present time, the action has been completed. Compare the following sentences.

> *I **saw** that movie yesterday.*
> *I **have seen** that movie.*

The first sentence, using *saw,* stresses a *past* action—what I did yesterday. The second stresses that I am currently experienced with that movie: I now know what it is about, that is, I *have* (present) *seen* (completed, finished with) that movie.

An idiomatic use of this tense is associated with the words *for* and *since.*

> *I **have tried for** three hours to phone him.*
> *I **have tried since** five o'clock to phone him.*

In the first sentence, the present perfect tense implies that there is a momentary lull, but the three hours of trying have lasted up to the present.

French Perfect (compound) tenses

Forms All perfect tenses in the active voice are formed with a single auxiliary and the past participle of the main verb. (See pages 83 and 85 for participle formation.)

Types In French, there is a perfect tense that corresponds to each of the simple (one-word) tenses. These perfect tenses are used much as their English counterparts, except for the first, the passé composé, since its use differs greatly from the English tense formed in the same way. One of these tenses will not be studied: the passé surcomposé, which is used only in literary works (see Appendix D).

French Passé composé

Forms The passé composé is formed with the present tense of the auxiliary verb plus the past participle of the main verb.

AUXILIARIES French, like German and Italian, has two possible auxiliary verbs. In fact, English had a second form at one time (*The hour is come*), but it is now considered obsolete.

Avoir is the more common French auxiliary and is used with a large majority of verbs. **Être** is used

1. with a small group of verbs (fewer than 20)—all intransitive, many expressing motion. Verbs that are formed from these verbs by adding a prefix also use *être* (for example, *venir → revenir, devenir, parvenir,* etc.).

   Some of these verbs may be used transitively. For example, *monter* can mean "to go up" (intransitive) or "to carry up" (transitive).

INTRANSITIVE	*Je **suis monté** au premier.*	I went up to the second floor.
TRANSITIVE	*J'**ai monté** l'escalier.*	I climbed the stairs.
	*J'**ai monté** ma valise.*	I carried my suitcase up.
INTRANSITIVE	*Elle **est sortie**.*	She went out.
TRANSITIVE	*Elle **a sorti** le livre de la bibliothèque.*	She took the book out of the library.

   Avoir must be used in sentences that have direct objects (that is, where the verb is transitive).

2. with any verb that is used reflexively or reciprocally.

*Nous nous **sommes rencontrés** à 5 heures.*	We met at five o'clock.
*Ils **se sont parlé**.*	They talked to each other.

   For help in remembering the verbs that commonly use *être* as their auxiliary, study the illustration on the next page.

CONTINUED ON PAGE 99 ▶

 Present perfect progressive tense

Definition All progressive tenses emphasize duration, and all are conjugated with the auxiliary verb *to be* plus the present participle of the main verb.

Forms The present perfect progressive tense in English uses *to be* in the present perfect with the main verb expressed by its present participle.

	SINGULAR	PLURAL
FIRST PERSON	*I have been singing*	*we have been singing*
SECOND PERSON	*you have been singing*	*you have been singing*
THIRD PERSON	*he/she has been singing*	*they have been singing*

Uses Like other progressive tenses, the present perfect progressive tense emphasizes duration. Consider the following sentences.

> *I **have tried** since five o'clock to phone him.*
> *I **have been trying** for three hours to phone him.*

The second sentence stresses how long the three hours have seemed to us.

La Maison d'être: Common verbs that use *être* as their auxiliary

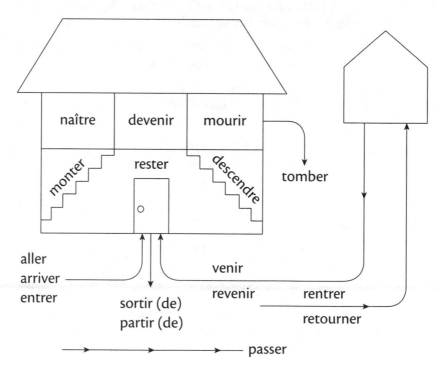

parler	finir	rendre	aller
j'ai parlé	j'ai fini	j'ai rendu	je suis allé(e)
tu as parlé	tu as fini	tu as rendu	tu es allé(e)
il/elle a parlé	il/elle a fini	il/elle a rendu	il/elle est allé(e)
nous avons parlé	nous avons fini	nous avons rendu	nous sommes allé(e)s
vous avez parlé	vous avez fini	vous avez rendu	vous êtes allé(e)(s)
ils/elles ont parlé	ils/elles ont fini	ils/elles ont rendu	ils/elles sont allé(e)s

AGREEMENT OF THE PAST PARTICIPLE When a past participle is used as an adjective, it agrees with the noun it modifies, as expected.

le français parlé	spoken French
objets trouvés	lost and found

When used as part of a perfect tense, the past participle follows one of two rules for agreement.

1. Intransitive verbs conjugated with *être* agree with the subject.

   Elle est **morte**.
   Nous sommes **venus**.

2. All other verbs agree with the direct object if it comes before the verb.

   *Voici **une maison**. Les Dupont **l'ont vendue** et c'est **celle** que Paul a **achetée**.*

   Care must be taken with reflexive pronoun objects. *Ils se sont **vus*** is clear, but some reflexive pronouns are indirect objects. In such cases, there is no agreement.

   *Ils se sont **dit** bonjour.*

 QUICK CHECK

The following rules apply to all perfect (compound) tenses, not just the passé composé.

USE OF THE CORRECT AUXILIARY	AGREEMENT OF THE PAST PARTICIPLE
être: some intransitive verbs of motion	Rule 1: agrees with the subject
être: any verb used reflexively or reciprocally	Rule 2: agrees with the direct object if it comes before the verb
avoir: all other verbs	Rule 2: agrees with its noun when used as an adjective

WORD ORDER The auxiliary verb—the one that is conjugated—typically fills the same position in the sentence that a simple-tense verb would hold, and the past participle is placed at the end.

 QUICK CHECK

Il le dit.	*Il l'a dit.*
Il ne le dit pas.	*Il ne l'a pas dit.*
Le dit-il?	*L'a-t-il dit?*
Ne le dit-il pas?	*Ne l'a-t-il pas dit?*

Uses The passé composé in French is used like the simple past tense in English—not like the present perfect tense, which looks like the passé composé. The passé composé refers to a completed action; the imperfect tense is used for other situations. (See page 91 for contrasting uses of these two tenses.)

 Past perfect (pluperfect) tense

Definition The past perfect tense indicates that some action (or state) was completed before some other past action (or state).

Forms The past perfect tense is formed with the simple past tense of the auxiliary verb *to have* plus the past participle of the main verb.

	SINGULAR	PLURAL
FIRST PERSON	*I had sung*	*we had sung*
SECOND PERSON	*you had sung*	*you had sung*
THIRD PERSON	*he/she had sung*	*they had sung*

These forms are often contracted to *I'd, you'd,* and so on.

*I'd **returned** the book before you **asked** for it.*

Uses Think of the past time sequence in terms of "yesterday" (past) and "last week" (further in the past).

*Mary **had finished** her homework before I **began** to talk to her.*
PAST PERFECT: last week   PAST: yesterday

 Past perfect progressive tense

Definition This tense shares characteristics with others that have been introduced. It is

1. past (in terms of time).

2. perfect (in the sense of "completed").

3. progressive (with stress on duration).

Forms The past perfect progressive tense is formed with the past perfect tense of the verb *to be* plus the present participle of the main verb.

	SINGULAR	PLURAL
FIRST PERSON	*I had been singing*	*we had been singing*
SECOND PERSON	*you had been singing*	*you had been singing*
THIRD PERSON	*he/she had been singing*	*they had been singing*

Uses This tense expresses an action (or state) that had been continuing just before another past action (or state).

*I **had been waiting** for three weeks when the letter **arrived**.*

That is, the wait started three weeks ago and continued up to yesterday, when the letter arrived.

French Past perfect (pluperfect) tense

Forms The past perfect tense in French is formed with the imperfect tense of the auxiliary (*avoir* or *être*) plus the past participle of the main verb.

parler	aller*
j'avais parlé	j'étais allé(e)
tu avais parlé	tu étais allé(e)
il/elle avait parlé	il/elle était allé(e)
nous avions parlé	nous étions allé(e)s
vous aviez parlé	vous étiez allé(e)(s)
ils/elles avaient parlé	ils/elles étaient allé(e)s

Uses Just as in English, the past perfect tense in French refers to an action or state completed further in the past than some other past action or state.

> *Marie **avait fini** son devoir, donc j'**ai commencé** à lui parler.*
> PAST PERFECT: last week   PAST: yesterday

---

*See page 99 for agreement of the past participle.

 # Future perfect tense

Definition   This tense expresses an action that will be completed at some time in the future.

Forms   The future perfect tense is formed with the future tense of the auxiliary *to have* plus the past participle of the main verb.

	SINGULAR	PLURAL
FIRST PERSON	*I will have sung*	*we will have sung*
SECOND PERSON	*you will have sung*	*you will have sung*
THIRD PERSON	*he/she will have sung*	*they will have sung*

These forms are often contracted, especially in speech, to *I'll've, you'll've,* and so on.

Uses   This tense is used to express future completion.

> *I **will have finished** the book before the professor **gives** an exam.*
> FUTURE PERFECT   PRESENT

In the second clause, the present tense is used in English, even though the verb refers to an action in the future; the professor is not giving an exam now.

 # Future perfect progressive tense

Definition   This tense expresses an action or state that will be continued and then completed in the future.

Forms   The future perfect progressive tense is formed with the future perfect tense of the auxiliary *to be* plus the present participle of the main verb.

	SINGULAR	PLURAL
FIRST PERSON	*I will have been singing*	*we will have been singing*
SECOND PERSON	*you will have been singing*	*you will have been singing*
THIRD PERSON	*he/she will have been singing*	*they will have been singing*

Uses   This tense is used to emphasize the duration of an action whose beginning point is not specified but whose completion (at least provisionally) will be in the future.

> *I **will have been studying** English for 16 years when I **graduate**.*
> FUTURE PERFECT PROGRESSIVE   PRESENT

Although graduation is in the future, English uses the present tense. The sentence does not indicate when the speaker will graduate, nor when he or she began to study English. The important point is the relationship between the verbs in the two clauses; 16 years of study will be completed at the moment in the future when I graduate.

Future perfect tense

Forms   The future perfect tense is formed with the auxiliary in the future tense plus the past participle.

parler	aller*
j'aurai parlé	je serai allé(e)
tu auras parlé	tu seras allé(e)
il/elle aura parlé	il/elle sera allé(e)
nous aurons parlé	nous serons allé(e)s
vous aurez parlé	vous serez allé(e)(s)
ils/elles auront parlé	ils/elles seront allé(e)s

Uses   The future perfect tense is used

1. as in English.

2. after *quand, lorsque, dès que,* and *aussitôt que* to express a future completed action, even though English uses the present tense (see page 88).

*Quand vous **viendrez**, j'**aurai terminé** mon travail.*	When you come (sometime in the future), I will have finished my work.
*Quand vous l'**aurez terminé**, nous le **discuterons**.*	When you have finished it (sometime in the future), we will discuss it.

---

*See page 99 for agreement of the past participle.

 **Conditional perfect tense**

Forms This tense is formed with the conditional tense of *to have* plus the past participle of the main verb.

	SINGULAR	PLURAL
FIRST PERSON	*I would have sung*	*we would have sung*
SECOND PERSON	*you would have sung*	*you would have sung*
THIRD PERSON	*he/she would have sung*	*they would have sung*

These forms are often contracted, especially in speech, to *I'd've, you'd've,* and so on.

I'd've come if **I'd** known.

Uses This tense is used primarily in the result clauses of Type 3 conditional sentences (see below).

He **would have seen** the film if he **had known** that it was so good.
We **would have come** if we   **had known** about it.
    CONDITIONAL PERFECT   PAST PERFECT

The *'d* in English can be a contraction of both *had* and *would*. This can cause some confusion unless the meaning of a sentence is analyzed.

If he**'d said** he needed it, I**'d have given** it to him.
    PLUPEFECT   CONDITIONAL PERFECT

 QUICK CHECK

THE THREE MOST COMMON TYPES OF CONDITIONAL SENTENCES IN ENGLISH

if-CLAUSE	RESULT CLAUSE	*if*-CLAUSE	RESULT CLAUSE
1. *If you* **are** *ready,*	*we* **will** *go.*	PRESENT	FUTURE
2. *If you* **were** *ready,*	*we* **would** *go.*	SUBJUNCTIVE	CONDITIONAL
3. *If you* **had been** *ready,*	*we* **would have** *gone.*	PLUPERFECT	CONDITIONAL PERFECT

English **Conditional perfect progressive tense**

Forms This tense is formed with the conditional perfect tense of the auxiliary *to be* plus the present participle of the main verb.

	SINGULAR	PLURAL
FIRST PERSON	*I would have been singing*	*we would have been singing*
SECOND PERSON	*you would have been singing*	*you would have been singing*
THIRD PERSON	*he/she would have been singing*	*they would have been singing*

Uses The conditional perfect progressive tense is used in the same way as the conditional perfect, except that the idea of duration is added.

I **would** not **have been sleeping** when you arrived, if I **had known** you were coming.
CONDITIONAL PERFECT PROGRESSIVE   PAST PERFECT

French Conditional perfect tense

Forms   This tense is formed with the conditional of the auxiliary plus the past participle of the main verb.

parler	aller
j'aurais parlé	je serais allé(e)
tu aurais parlé	tu serais allé(e)
il/elle/on aurait parlé	il/elle/on serait allé(e)
nous aurions parlé	nous serions allé(e)s
vous auriez parlé	vous seriez allé(e)(s)
ils/elles auraient parlé	ils/elles seraient allé(e)s

Uses   In French, the conditional perfect tense is used, as in English, primarily for Type 3 conditional sentences.

Il **aurait vu** le film s'il   **avait su** qu'il était si bon.
    CONDITIONAL PERFECT   PLUPERFECT

Nous **serions venus** si nous en **avions su** quelque chose.
    CONDITIONAL PERFECT   PLUPERFECT

 QUICK CHECK

THE THREE TYPES OF CONDITIONAL SENTENCES IN FRENCH

if-CLAUSE	RESULT CLAUSE	if-CLAUSE	RESULT CLAUSE
1. Si vous **êtes** prêt,	nous **irons**.	PRESENT	FUTURE
2. Si vous **étiez** prêt,	nous **irions**.	IMPERFECT	CONDITIONAL
3. Si vous **aviez été** prêt,	nous y **serions allés**.	PLUPERFECT	CONDITIONAL PERFECT

English Passive voice

Definition   The passive voice is used when the subject receives the action of the verb.

ACTIVE VOICE	*The dog*	*bit*	*Susie.*
	SUBJECT	ACTIVE VERB	DIRECT OBJECT
PASSIVE VOICE	*Susie*	*was bitten*	*by the dog.*
	SUBJECT	PASSIVE VERB	AGENT

Notice that the direct object of the active verb becomes the subject of the passive verb. The active verb's subject is placed after the passive verb in a prepositional phrase and is called the agent. It is not always expressed, as in the colloquial *John got caught*; for such a sentence, it is either not important or not known by whom or what John was caught.

Forms   The passive voice is formed with *to be* or *to get* plus the past participle of the main verb.

Only transitive verbs (ones that have a direct object) can be made passive.

PRESENT	ACTIVE	*John catches the ball.*
	PASSIVE	*The ball is caught by John.*
PAST	ACTIVE	*The man read the book.*
	PASSIVE	*The book was read by the man.*
FUTURE	ACTIVE	*Mrs. Smith will lead the discussion.*
	PASSIVE	*The discussion will be led by Mrs. Smith.*
CONDITIONAL PERFECT	ACTIVE	*The class would have finished the job, but . . .*
	PASSIVE	*The job would have been finished by the class, but . . .*

All the perfect and progressive tenses of the passive voice are formed in the same way. Some forms can be very long and are seldom used; an example of the passive future progressive follows.

*The work **will have been being done** at 3 P.M.*

French Passive voice

Forms The passive voice in French is formed with the verb *être* plus the past participle of the main verb acting like an adjective, that is, agreeing with the subject. The passive voice is used in all tenses.

Agency (expressed with English "by") is usually expressed by *par* in French, although *de* is sometimes used.

PRESENT	ACTIVE	*Jean **attrape** la balle.*
	PASSIVE	*La balle **est attrapée** par Jean.*
PASSÉ COMPOSÉ	ACTIVE	*L'homme **a lu** le livre.*
	PASSIVE	*Le livre **a été lu** par l'homme.*

In French, the passive voice in all tenses is formed with the appropriate tense of *être* plus the past participle of the main verb.

Uses The French prefer the active voice to the passive. (English teachers often suggest using the passive voice as a way of improving one's writing, and authors sometimes even tend to use less vivid language when writing in the passive.) Compare the following English sentences.

PASSIVE   *Our receiver was tackled by their defensive end.*
ACTIVE   *Their defensive end slammed our receiver to the ground.*

PASSIVE   *This abstract was painted by Pablo Picasso.*
ACTIVE   *Pablo Picasso created this colorful abstract.*

If speakers of English are less than enthusiastic about the passive, the French actively dislike it. As a result, it is seldom used. There are a number of ways to avoid the passive voice in French.

1. Turn the sentence around.

   NOT *Le livre a été lu par la classe.*
   BUT *La classe a lu le livre.*

2. Use *on.*

   NOT *Le français est parlé ici.*
   BUT *Ici on parle français.*

3. Use the reflexive.

   NOT *Hier les robes étaient vendues à bas prix.*
   BUT *Hier les robes se vendaient à bas prix.*

English Imperative mood

Definition The imperative mood is the mood used to give commands.

Forms The forms of the English imperative are very similar to those of the present indicative, with a few exceptions.

The second-person imperative (both singular and plural) has only one form: *Sing!*

For the first-person plural, the auxiliary verb *let* is used.

> *Let's sing!*

For the third-person (singular and plural), the auxiliary verbs *let, have,* and *make* are used.

> *Let her sing!*
> *Have them come in!*
> *Make him stop!*

No subject is expressed in an imperative sentence.

IRREGULAR IMPERATIVES English has only one irregular imperative: for the verb *to be.* Compare the following sentences.

INDICATIVE	IMPERATIVE
You are good.	*Be good!*
We are quiet.	*Let's be quiet!*

French Imperative mood

Forms   The imperative mood in French has three forms: the second-person familiar, the second-person formal, and the first-person plural (the *let's* form in English). These forms are the same as those of the indicative except that

1. the subject is not expressed.

2. the *-s* drops from the ending of *-er* verbs in the singular.

	parler	*finir*	*dormir*	*rendre*
SECOND-PERSON FAMILIAR	*parle!*	*finis!*	*dors!*	*rends!*
SECOND-PERSON FORMAL	*parlez!*	*finissez!*	*dormez!*	*rendez!*
FIRST-PERSON PLURAL	*parlons!*	*finissons!*	*dormons!*	*rendons!*

In the second-person familiar imperative form, the second-person singular *-s* ending of *-er* verbs is retained before the object pronouns *y* and *en*.

> **Vas**-*y.*
> **Parles**-*en un peu.*

For the third-person command, the subjunctive mood is used (see pages 111 and 113–114). The notion "I want" is understood.

> *Qu'elle* **entre**!   Let her enter! (= I want her to enter.)
> *Qu'ils* **soient** *tranquilles!*   Make them be quiet! (= I want them to be quiet.)

IRREGULAR IMPERATIVES   Only four French verbs have irregular forms in the imperative mood.

	avoir	*être*	*savoir*	*vouloir*
SECOND-PERSON FAMILIAR	*aie*	*sois*	*sache*	—
SECOND-PERSON FORMAL	*ayez*	*soyez*	*sachez*	*veuillez*
FIRST-PERSON PLURAL	*ayons*	*soyons*	*sachons*	—

Veuillez is the form used to make a request.

> **Veuillez** *être à l'heure demain.*   Please be on time tomorrow.

WORD ORDER   In affirmative commands, pronoun objects follow the verb and are attached to it by a hyphen. The direct object always precedes the indirect object (see page 27).

> *Donnez-le-moi!*   Give it to me!
> *Dites-le-lui!*   Say it to him!

In negative commands, the objects are in their normal position and order.

> *Ne me le donnez pas!*   Don't give it to me!
> *Ne le lui dites pas!*   Don't say it to him.

English Subjunctive mood

Definition   The subjunctive is the mood that expresses what may be true.

Forms   The **present subjunctive** (or the auxiliary verb in a compound tense) has the same form for all persons: the basic (infinitive) form of the verb. It is different from the indicative only for

1. the third-person singular.

   that he take
   that she have

2. the verb *to be*.

   PRESENT   *that I be, that he be*
   PAST   *that I were, that she were*

CONTINUED ON PAGE 112 ▶

French Subjunctive mood

Forms Subjunctive tenses are fully conjugated in French. (Only the present and past tenses of the subjunctive are presented here; the imperfect and pluperfect subjunctive tenses are rarely used.) The **present subjunctive** is formed as follows.

STEM   Drop the *-ent* of the third-person plural of the present indicative form.
ENDINGS   Add *-e, -es, -e; -ions, -iez, -ent.*

The subjunctive forms of most *-er* verbs are exactly like the indicative forms except for the first- and second-person plural.

parler (*ils/elles parlent*)	*finir* (*ils/elles finissent*)	*dormir* (*ils/elles dorment*)	*rendre* (*ils/elles rendent*)
que je parle	*que je finisse*	*que je dorme*	*que je rende*
que tu parles	*que tu finisses*	*que tu dormes*	*que tu rendes*
qu'il/elle parle	*qu'il/elle finisse*	*qu'il/elle dorme*	*qu'il/elle rende*
que nous parlions	*que nous finissions*	*que nous dormions*	*que nous rendions*
que vous parliez	*que vous finissiez*	*que vous dormiez*	*que vous rendiez*
qu'ils/elles parlent	*qu'ils/elles finissent*	*qu'ils/elles dorment*	*qu'ils/elles rendent*

Que is placed before the subjunctive forms above to show that these forms are used only in subordinate clauses (even if the main clause is not expressed).

IRREGULAR SUBJUNCTIVES Only two French verbs have irregular endings in the present subjunctive.

avoir	*être*
que j'aie	*que je sois*
que tu aies	*que tu sois*
qu'il/elle ait	*qu'il/elle soit*
que nous ayons	*que nous soyons*
que vous ayez	*que vous soyez*
qu'ils/elles aient	*qu'ils/elles soient*

Other verbs have an irregular stem but use the regular subjunctive endings.

pouvoir → *que je **puisse***
avoir   → *que je **sache***
faire   → *que je **fosse***
falloir → *qu'il **faille*** (only used in the third-person singular)

In addition, a number of verbs that change the stem for the *nous* and *vous* forms in the present indicative also change the stem in the present subjunctive.

INFINITIVE	BASIC STEM	*nous/vous* STEM
aller	*que j'aille*	*que nous allions*
vouloir	*que je veuille*	*que nous voulions*
boire	*que je boive*	*que nous buvions*
venir	*que je vienne*	*que nous venions*

The **past subjunctive** is easily recognized, since its forms are the same as those for the passé composé except that the auxiliary verb is in the present subjunctive.

*que j'**aie parlé***
*qu'elle **soit venue***

CONTINUED ON PAGE 113 ▶

Uses The subjunctive is rarely used in English. For that reason, it tends to be disregarded except in certain fixed expressions. Nevertheless, it does have some specific uses that are important in formal English.

1. In contrary-to-fact conditions

   *If I **were** you . . .*
   *"If this **be** madness, yet there is method in it." (Hamlet)*

2. After verbs like *wish, suppose, insist, urge, demand, ask, recommend,* and *suggest*

   *I wish that he **were** able to come.*
   *They insisted that we **be** present.*
   *I recommend that she **learn** the subjunctive.*

3. After some impersonal expressions, such as *it is necessary* and *it is important*

   *It is important that he **avoid** errors.*
   *It is necessary that Mary **see** its importance.*

4. In certain fixed expressions

   *So **be** it!*
   *Long **live** the Queen!*
   *Heaven **forbid**!*
   *Far **be** it from me to suggest that!*

   Most of these fixed expressions express a third-person imperative; the idea "I wish that" is implied, but not expressed.

   Except for the fixed expressions, English speakers tend to use an alternative expression whenever possible, usually with modal verbs (auxiliaries), to avoid the subjunctive in conversation and informal writing. Compare the following sentences with the examples above.

   *I wish that he **could come**.*
   *I told her that she **must learn** the subjunctive.*
   *It is important for him **to avoid** errors.*
   *Mary **needs to see** its importance.*

Uses In theory, the subjunctive is used to express that something is

1. potentially (but not actually) true.

2. colored by emotion (which often distorts facts).

3. an attitude about something (rather than an actual fact).

4. doubtful, probably nonexistent, or simply untrue.

In practice, there are certain words and expressions that require the subjunctive. Theory may help a French learner remember which ones require the subjunctive, but theory must yield to practice. If an expression requires the subjunctive, it must be used, whether or not one believes that it accords with theory.

The subjunctive is used principally

1. after verbs and expressions conveying the subject's emotional reactions.

> *je suis **content** que...*
> *il **craint** que...*
> *elles **regrettent** que...*

2. after verbs such as *vouloir, supposer, exiger,* and *demander* when there is a change of subject.

> ***Je** veux qu'**il** vienne.*
> ***Je** veux venir.*

In the second example above, the infinitive is used because there is no change of subject.

3. after impersonal expressions when uncertainty is conveyed. Compare the following lists of expressions.

FOLLOWED BY A SUBJUNCTIVE VERB	FOLLOWED BY AN INDICATIVE VERB
il est peu probable que	*il est probable que*
il est possible que	*il est vrai que*
il est incroyable que	*il est certain que*
il semble que	*il me semble que*
il est étonnant que	*il paraît que*
il est souhaitable que	
il est bon que	
il vaut mieux que	

4. after conjunctions expressing the following ideas.

CONCESSION	*quoique, bien que*
PURPOSE	*pour que, afin que*
INDEFINITE TIME	*jusqu'à ce que, avant que*
NEGATION	*sans que, à moins que*

CONTINUED ON PAGE 114 ▶

5. after superlatives (because of the possibility of exaggeration). Compare the following sentences.

> *C'est le plus beau poème que je **connaisse**.* (a personal opinion, therefore subjunctive)
> *New York est la plus grande ville que j'ai jamais **visitée**.* (a fact, therefore indicative)

The first sentence expresses an emotion, the second expresses a fact; the subjunctive and indicative signal how a statement is meant to be understood. Some native French speakers do not make this distinction and use the subjunctive in every case.

6. after certain verbs (especially *penser* and *croire*) in the negative and interrogative. (Asking what someone thinks, or saying what someone does not believe, implies doubt about the actual situation.) The negative-interrogative *Ne pensez-vous pas que...?* often takes the indicative because a positive response is expected.

7. in third-person commands (see page 109).

8. in certain fixed expressions.

> *Vive le roi!*
> *À Dieu ne plaise!*

To remember the principal uses of the subjunctive in French, the mnemonic "**SWAP NEEDS**" may be used.

Seeming
Wishing
Asking
Possibility
Necessity
Emotion
Exaggeration
Demanding
Supposing

How to avoid the subjunctive in French

The subjunctive is used only in subordinate clauses (even if the main clause is not expressed) and only when the subjects of the two clauses are different. If the subject is the same, you may avoid the subjunctive by using

1. the infinitive. Compare the following sentences.

> *Je suis content que **vous soyez** ici.* (different subjects)
> *Je suis content d'être ici.* (same subject)

2. an impersonal expression with an indirect object pronoun. Compare the following sentences.

> *Il faut que je parte.*
> *Il me faut partir.* (not as common in everyday use)

Exercises

The following exercises, grouped by part of speech, test your grasp of key grammatical aspects of French. As a reminder of the similarities and differences between French and English, a cross-reference is provided at the end of each exercise to the relevant grammar points discussed in this book. An answer key is provided after the appendices.

Nouns

A *Add the correct definite article before each of the following French nouns.*

1. _____ heure

2. _____ maison

3. _____ fleurs

4. _____ jeu

5. _____ jeux

6. _____ gens

7. _____ vin

8. _____ stylos

9. _____ ordinateur

10. _____ porte

◀ *For more help, see* Determiners, *pages 17–18.*

B *Add the correct indefinite article before each of the following French nouns.*

1. _____ mur

2. _____ salle de bains

3. _____ fenêtres

4. _____ porte

5. _____ clé

6. _____ chambres

7. _____ toit

8. _____ machine à laver

9. _____ balcons

10. _____ jardin

◀ For more help, see Determiners, *pages 17–18*.

C *Complete each of the following sentences with the correct determiner.*

1. Tu as soif? Voilà _____ café.

2. Où est _____ café?

3. J'achète _____ viande pour ce soir.

4. Et moi, j'achète _____ poisson.

5. Tu ne prends pas _____ légumes?

6. Non, mais je vais acheter _____ fruits.

7. _____ légumes sont bons pour _____ santé.

8. _____ fruits aussi.

9. Si on prenait _____ tarte aux poires à _____ pâtisserie du coin?

10. C'est _____ bonne idée. C'est _____ dessert excellent.

◀ For more help, see Determiners, *pages 17–18*.

Pronouns

A *Complete each of the following sentences with the correct subject pronoun.*

1. _____ n'ai pas mon livre aujourd'hui.

2. Qu'est-ce qu'_____ font, ces étudiantes?

3. Qu'est-ce que _____ désirez?

4. Où est-ce que _____ vas?

5. Marc ne sait pas s'_____ va venir avec nous.

6. _____ parlons avec eux tous les jours.

7. _____ ne sont pas là, les garçons?

8. Christine a faim. _____ va manger.

9. _____ vais en ville.

10. Est-ce que _____ parles anglais?

◀ For more help, see Personal pronouns, *page 23*.

B *Rewrite each of the following sentences, replacing the italicized direct object noun with the corresponding direct object pronoun.*

1. Elle lit *l'article.*   _____

2. Nous voulons louer *cet appartement.*   _____

3. Il prend *la bicyclette.*   _____

4. Ne perds pas *les billets.*   _____

5. Elles écrivent *leur adresse.*   _____

6. Nettoyons *notre chambre.*   _____

7. Ils peuvent comprendre *le texte.*   _____

8. Tu copies *les nouveaux mots.*   _____

9. Gardez *vos livres.*   _____

10. Vous vendez *la maison.*   _____

◀ *For more help, see* Personal pronouns, *page 23.*

C *Complete each of the following exchanges with the correct direct object pronoun.*

1. —Est-ce que vous me connaissez?

   —Non, je ne _____ connais pas.

2. —Il va t'inviter?

   —Je ne sais pas s'il va _____ inviter.

3. —Elle vous écrit à vous deux?

   —Oui, elle _____ écrit toutes les semaines.

4. —Je te dérange?

   —Non, tu ne _____ déranges pas du tout.

5. —Tu sais si Luc veut me parler?

   —Oui, il _____ cherche.

◀ *For more help, see* Personal pronouns, *page 23.*

D *Rewrite each of the following sentences, replacing the italicized words with the correct direct or indirect object pronouns or with* y *or* en. *Many of the sentences will have two object pronouns.*

1. Elles envoient *des cadeaux à leurs parents.*   _____

2. Je téléphone *à mon amie.*   _____

3. Donnez *de l'eau aux enfants.*   _____

4. Il travaille *au deuxième étage.*   _____

5. Veux-tu *du vin?*   _____

6. Il enseigne *le français aux enfants.* _____

7. Il enseigne *les langues dans ce lycée.* _____

8. Nous offrons *des bijoux à nos amies.* _____

9. Donnez-moi *de la salade,* s'il vous plaît. _____

10. Je vais mettre *les paquets sur la table.* _____

11. Nous te voyons toujours *dans ce café.* _____

12. Explique-t-elle *la leçon à leurs amies?* _____

◀ *For more help, see* Personal pronouns, *pages 23 and 25.*

E *Complete each of the following sentences with the correct disjunctive pronoun.*

1. Je ne viens pas, _____.

2. _____, ils travaillent dans l'informatique.

3. Vous avez tort, _____.

4. _____, elle parle bien l'anglais.

5. _____, tu es en retard.

6. Il se trompe toujours, _____.

7. Marie et Christine m'ont invité chez _____.

8. Mes parents et moi, nous vous invitons à dîner avec _____.

◀ *For more help, see* Disjunctive pronouns, *page 31.*

F *Complete the following French sentences so that they match the English sentences in meaning.*

1. I like my bicycle, but he prefers his.

   Moi, j'aime ma bicyclette, mais lui, il préfère _____.

2. This house is older than ours.

   Cette maison est plus vieille que _____.

3. These aren't Marie's books, they're mine.

   Ces livres ne sont pas à Marie, ce sont _____.

4. I have my CDs. Do you have yours?

   Moi, j'ai mes cédés. Tu as _____, toi?

5. She needs my pencil, because she has lost hers.

   Elle a besoin de mon crayon parce qu'elle a perdu _____.

6. My car is broken down. Can you take yours?

   Ma voiture est en panne. Pouvez-vous prendre _____?

7. I brought my photos, and they brought theirs.

Moi, j'ai apporté mes photos, et eux, ils ont apporté _____.

8. Our dog is bigger than theirs.

Notre chien est plus grand que _____.

◀ *For more help, see* Possessive pronouns, *page 27.*

G *Select the correct relative pronoun to complete each of the following sentences.*

1. Voilà l'article _____ j'ai lu.
   a. qui
   b. que
   c. ce qui
   d. ce que
   e. où

2. Je vais te montrer le bureau _____ j'ai travaillé avant.
   a. qui
   b. que
   c. ce qui
   d. ce que
   e. où

3. Le restaurant _____ est au coin est excellent.
   a. qui
   b. que
   c. ce qui
   d. ce que
   e. où

4. Nous ne comprenons pas _____ tu veux.
   a. qui
   b. que
   c. ce qui
   d. ce que
   e. où

5. Voilà la pâtisserie _____ j'achète mes bonbons.
   a. qui
   b. que
   c. ce qui
   d. ce que
   e. où

6. C'est _____ nous a surpris.
   a. qui
   b. que
   c. ce qui
   d. ce que
   e. où

7. C'est un thème _____ nous intéresse.
   a. qui
   b. que
   c. ce qui
   d. ce que
   e. où

8. L'ingénieur _____ vous connaissez est très intelligent.
   a. qui
   b. que
   c. ce qui
   d. ce que
   e. où

◀ *For more help, see* Relative pronouns, *page 33.*

H   *Translate the following phrases and sentences into French, using demonstrative pronouns.*

1. This book and that one.

   _____

2. My house and my sister's.

   _____

3. These restaurants are good, but those are better.

   _____

4. Your (*vous*) course and the one that we're taking (*suivre*) are excellent.

   _____

5. She is the one he loves.

   _____

6. These gardens and those.

   _____

7. Do you (*tu*) want those pastries or these?

   _____

8. We can take my car. Marie's is not big enough.

   _____

◀ *For more help, see* Demonstrative pronouns, *page 37.*

I *Complete each of the following French sentences with the missing interrogative pronoun so that the sentence matches the English sentence in meaning.*

1. Whom are you writing to?

   _____ est-ce que vous écrivez?

2. What are you looking for?

   _____ cherchez-vous?

3. What are they saying?

   _____ ils disent?

4. I like these two cars. Which is less expensive?

   J'aime ces deux voitures. _____ est moins chère?

5. What is the child afraid of?

   _____ est-ce que l'enfant a peur?

6. Whom is she going out with?

   _____ est-ce qu'elle sort?

7. What are you thinking about?

   _____ penses-tu?

8. There are so many newspapers. Which ones do you read?

   Il y a tant de journaux. _____ lisez-vous?

9. Who works there?

   _____ travaille là?

10. What did you do?

    _____ tu as fait?

11. Whom did you see?

    _____ tu as vu?

12. What's happening?

    _____ arrive?

13. Whom are these gifts for?

    _____ sont ces cadeaux?

14. Here are two software packages. Which one do you need?

    Voilà deux logiciels. _____ est-ce que vous avez besoin?

◀ *For more help, see* Interrogative pronouns, *pages 39–40.*

Adjectives

A   Complete the following lists with the missing forms of the adjective.

1. a. un livre _____

   b. une histoire _____

   c. des livres __intéressants__

   d. des histoires _____

2. a. un arbre __blanc__

   b. une fleur _____

   c. des arbres _____

   d. des fleurs _____

3. a. un homme _____

   b. une femme _____

   c. des hommes __fiers__

   d. des femmes _____

4. a. un endroit __merveilleux__

   b. une ville _____

   c. des endroits _____

   d. des villes _____

5. a. un _____ livre

   b. une _____ voiture

   c. des __gros__ livres

   d. des _____ voitures

6. a. un garçon _____

   b. une fille _____

   c. des garçons _____

   d. des filles __heureuses__

7. a. un homme __actif__

   b. une femme _____

   c. des hommes _____

   d. des femmes _____

8. a. un monument __national__

   b. une équipe _____

   c. des monuments _____

   d. des équipes _____

9. a. un restaurant _italien_

    b. une recette _____

    c. des restaurants _____

    d. des recettes _____

10. a. un paquet _léger_

    b. une valise _____

    c. des paquets _____

    d. des valises _____

◀ For more help, see Descriptive adjectives, page 44.

B *Complete each of the following sentences with the correct form of* nouveau.

1. J'ai de _____ chaussures.

2. C'est un _____ film.

3. J'aime ta _____ voiture.

4. Nous avons un _____ ordinateur.

5. Tu as de _____ projets?

6. C'est un _____ immeuble.

◀ For more help, see Descriptive adjectives, page 44.

C *Complete each of the following sentences with the correct form of* beau.

1. Vous avez un _____ appartement.

2. C'est un très _____ livre.

3. Il a une _____ femme.

4. Lui, c'est un _____ homme.

5. Ils ont de _____ enfants.

6. Il y a beaucoup de _____ maisons dans ce quartier.

◀ For more help, see Descriptive adjectives, page 44.

D *Complete each of the following sentences with the correct form of* vieux.

1. J'aime bien la _____ ville.

2. Ce sont nos _____ amis.

3. Son père est déjà un _____ homme.

4. C'est une charmante _____ dame.

5. J'ai toujours mon _____ ordinateur.

6. Il adore les _____ voitures.

◀ *For more help, see* Descriptive adjectives, *page 44.*

E *Translate the following phrases into French.*

1. a poor (unfortunate) man _____

2. a dear friend [fem.] _____

3. a former general _____

4. an ancient city _____

5. a great woman _____

6. a poor (penniless) man _____

7. a tall girl _____

8. an expensive car _____

◀ *For more help, see* Descriptive adjectives, *page 45.*

F *Translate the following sentences into French.*

1. Jacques is more intelligent than Marc.

_____

2. My sister is less happy than my brother.

_____

3. It's the best book in the library.

_____

4. The subway is faster than the bus.

_____

5. He is the worst student at the lycée.

_____

6. My course is less interesting than their course.

_____

◀ *For more help, see* Comparison of adjectives, *page 47.*

G *Complete each of the following sentences with the correct form of the demonstrative adjective.*

1. Connaissez-vous _____ homme?

2. _____ idées m'intéressent.

3. _____ faculté a une très bonne réputation.

4. Vous avez déjà mangé dans _____ restaurant?

5. _____ article est très important.

6. Qui est _____ monsieur?

7. _____ étudiants sont très diligents.

8. _____ lacs sont très beaux.

◀ *For more help, see* Demonstrative adjectives, *page 49.*

H *Translate the following phrases into French.*

1. her book   _____

2. my school   _____

3. his house   _____

4. our translation   _____

5. their gardens   _____

6. your [familiar] ideas _____

7. your (*vous*) notebooks _____

8. my homework assignments _____

9. your [familiar] poster _____

10. his story   _____

◀ *For more help, see* Possessive adjectives, *page 51.*

I *Complete each of the following questions and exclamations with the correct form of* quel.

1. _____ chemise allez-vous mettre?

2. _____ travail difficile!

3. Vous allez à _____ magasin?

4. _____ bâtiment magnifique!

5. _____ journaux aimez-vous?

6. _____ traductions sont bonnes?

7. _____ jeux aiment-ils?

8. _____ pièce ennuyeuse!

◀ *For more help, see* Interrogative adjectives, *page 51.*

Adverbs

A *Write the adverb that corresponds to each of the following adjectives.*

1. facile _____
2. actif _____
3. merveilleux _____
4. bon _____
5. lent _____
6. clair _____
7. vif _____
8. certain _____
9. soigneux _____
10. vague _____

◀ *For more help, see* Introducing adverbs, *page 57.*

Negatives

A *Translate the following negative sentences into French.*

1. He doesn't work. _____
2. He doesn't work anymore. _____
3. He never works. _____
4. No one works. _____
5. She is not learning anything. _____
6. We don't see Christine or Marie. _____

◀ *For more help, see* Introducing adverbs, *page 59.*

Prepositions

A *Add the correct preposition before each of the following geographical names.*

1. Ils ont une maison _____ Californie.
2. Cet été je vais aller _____ France.
3. J'ai trouvé un travail _____ Paris.
4. Ses amis sont _____ Canada maintenant.

5. Ils sont _____ Montréal.

6. J'ai un oncle _____ États-Unis.

7. Il travaille _____ Nouvelle Orléans.

8. Je ne sais pas s'il va revenir _____ Europe.

◀ *For more help, see* Introducing prepositions, *page 73.*

B *Add the correct preposition before the infinitive in each of the following sentences.*
If no preposition is required, write an X.

1. Elle continue _____ étudier le français.

2. Tu dois _____ faire attention à ta santé.

3. Il semble _____ être inquiet.

4. J'ai décidé _____ changer de travail.

5. Nous regrettons _____ vous dire que nous ne pourrons pas venir.

6. Il m'a invité _____ l'accompagner.

7. Elle refuse _____ répondre.

8. Il faut _____ l'acheter.

9. Je crois _____ vous connaître.

10. Ils ont oublié _____ nous appeler.

11. Elle apprend _____ programmer.

12. Ils essaient _____ nous convaincre.

◀ *For more help, see* Introducing prepositions, *page 74.*

Questions

A *Turn the following sentences into questions using inversion.*

1. Jean achète des livres.   _____

2. Nous avons dîné ici.   _____

3. Vous suivez cette route.   _____

4. Il les a pris.   _____

5. Carole vous a téléphoné.   _____

◀ *For more help, see* Introducing questions, *page 79.*

Verbs

A   *Complete the following chart with the present and past participles of each infinitive.*

INFINITIVE	PRESENT PARTICIPLE	PAST PARTICIPLE
1. marcher	_____	_____
2. choisir	_____	_____
3. avoir	_____	_____
4. descendre	_____	_____
5. lire	_____	_____
6. mentir	_____	_____
7. être	_____	_____
8. sourire	_____	_____
9. balayer	_____	_____
10. nettoyer	_____	_____
11. acheter	_____	_____
12. préférer	_____	_____
13. prendre	_____	_____
14. savoir	_____	_____
15. ouvrir	_____	_____
16. réfléchir	_____	_____
17. boire	_____	_____
18. faire	_____	_____
19. recevoir	_____	_____
20. dire	_____	_____
21. mettre	_____	_____
22. pouvoir	_____	_____
23. voir	_____	_____
24. écrire	_____	_____

◀ *For more help, see* Participles, *pages 83 and 85.*

B   *Complete each of the following sentences with the correct present tense form of the verb in parentheses.*

1. (marcher)   Ils _____ vite.

2. (choisir)   Nous _____ des cadeaux de Noël.

3. (descendre)   Je _____ faire les courses.

4. (mentir)   Cet enfant _____ toujours.

5. (finir)   Elle _____ ses devoirs avant de sortir.

6. (sortir)   Elle _____ à sept heures et demie.

7. (chanter)   Tu _____ bien.

8. (vendre)   Qui _____ ses livres?

9. (courir)   Je _____ un peu tous les jours.

10. (dormir)   Combien d'heures _____-tu chaque nuit?

11. (louer)   Vous _____ beaucoup de films.

12. (servir)   Qu'est-ce qu'ils _____ ce soir?

13. (réfléchir)   Vous _____ à votre avenir.

14. (partir)   Elles _____ demain.

15. (rendre)   Il _____ les livres à la bibliothèque.

◀ *For more help, see* Present tense, *page 87.*

C   *Translate the following sentences into French.*

1. Where is he going?

_____

2. I always walk in the morning.

_____

3. Where do they [fem.] work?

_____

4. We have been waiting for an hour.

_____

5. I don't know where he is.

_____

6. Washington, D.C. is the capital of the United States.

_____

7. I am leaving for Paris next week.

_____

8. He speaks Spanish.

_____

◀ *For more help, see* Present tense, *pages 87 and 89.*

D *Rewrite the following sentences, using the imperfect tense.*

1. Il parle avec sa fiancée. _____
2. Nous finissons notre travail. _____
3. Elle prend un café. _____
4. J'attends mes amis. _____
5. L'enfant dort. _____
6. Nous sommes pressés. _____
7. Tu vends ta maison. _____
8. Elle travaille dans ce bureau. _____
9. Nous étudions nos leçons. _____
10. Il faut partir. _____
11. Ils vont en ville. _____
12. Je fais mes devoirs. _____
13. Tu écris une lettre. _____
14. Vous lisez beaucoup. _____
15. Je sors. _____
16. Elle est en ville. _____
17. Le professeur efface le tableau. _____
18. Tu manges à une heure. _____

◀ *For more help, see* Past tenses (imperfect tense), *page 91.*

E *Complete each of the following sentences with the correct future tense form of the verb in parentheses.*

1. (aller)   Il _____ en Europe.
2. (avoir)   J'_____ beaucoup à faire.
3. (prendre) Nous _____ un café ensemble.
4. (sortir)   Quand _____-tu?
5. (passer)   Je _____ te prendre à deux heures.
6. (choisir) Demain nous _____ nos cours.
7. (rendre)   Quand est-ce que vous me _____ l'argent?
8. (devoir)   Nous _____ l'inviter.
9. (envoyer) Je t'_____ un message électronique.
10. (réussir) Elle _____ à ses examens.
11. (être)   Vous _____ avec nous.
12. (pouvoir) Ils _____ vous accompagner.

13. (falloir)   Qu'est-ce qu'il _____ faire?

14. (arriver)   Quand est-ce que tu _____ ?

15. (attendre)   Vous m'_____, n'est-ce pas?

16. (finir)   Elles _____ le travail la semaine prochaine.

17. (nettoyer)   Nous _____ la cuisine.

18. (acheter)   Qu'est-ce qu'ils _____ ?

◀ For more help, see Future tense, page 93.

F *Rewrite the following sentences to express future time, using the present tense of* aller *+ the infinitive of the verb.*

1. Nous sortons.   _____

2. Elles arrivent demain. _____

3. Il vient avec eux.   _____

4. Je monte.   _____

5. Ils voient ce film.   _____

6. Tu me téléphones.   _____

7. Vous comprenez.   _____

8. Nous sommes en retard. _____

9. Tu commandes un thé.   _____

10. Je passe te voir.   _____

◀ For more help, see Future tense, page 93.

G *Complete each of the following sentences with the correct conditional form of the verb in parentheses.*

1. (avoir)   Je croyais que les enfants _____ faim.

2. (préférer) Si j'avais le choix, je _____ l'autre costume.

3. (jeter)   Elle savait qu'il _____ sa lettre à la poubelle.

4. (faire)   Ils _____ du français s'ils pouvaient.

5. (rendre)   Si nous avions le temps, nous vous _____ visite.

6. (choisir)   Si vous pouviez recommencer, quel cours _____ -vous?

7. (voir)   Ils ont dit qu'ils _____ ce film avec nous.

8. (enlever)   S'il faisait chaud, j'_____ ma veste.

9. (balayer)   J'ai dit que je _____ le salon.

10. (être)   Nous pensions qu'ils _____ là.

◀ For more help, see Conditional tense, page 95.

H Complete each of the following sentences with the correct passé composé form of the verb in parentheses.

1. (servir)   Ils _____ un repas merveilleux.

2. (commencer)   L'enfant _____ à rire.

3. (nager)   J'_____ pendant une heure.

4. (entrer)   Elle _____ dans la salle de classe.

5. (laver)   Mon père _____ la voiture.

6. (déjeuner)   Nous _____ en ville.

7. (sortir)   Jacques et Pierre _____.

8. (apporter)   Vous m'_____ le journal?

9. (mourir)   Notre chien _____ hier.

10. (naître)   Leur fille _____ la semaine passée.

11. (prendre)   Nous _____ un café avec elle.

12. (vendre)   Ils _____ leur maison.

13. (réfléchir)   Est-ce que vous _____ au problème?

14. (organiser)   Tu _____ une réunion.

15. (retourner)   Elles _____ avec leurs parents.

16. (se laver)   Ils _____ avant de manger.

17. (demander)   Tu leur _____ de l'argent.

18. (mincir)   Je vois que tu _____.

◀ *For more help, see* Passé composé, *pages 97 and 99.*

I Answer each of the following questions, using the past perfect (pluperfect) tense and the word déjà, *as in the model.*

MODÈLE   Il voulait dîner?   *Il avait déjà dîné.*

1. Elle voulait descendre?   _____

2. Tu voulais accepter?   _____

3. Ils voulaient jouer?   _____

4. Elles voulaient rentrer?   _____

5. Vous vouliez parler, vous deux?   _____

6. Tu voulais téléphoner?   _____

7. Ils voulaient partir?   _____

8. Vous vouliez y réfléchir, vous deux?   _____

◀ *For more help, see* Past perfect (pluperfect) tense, *page 101.*

J Complete each of the following sentences with the correct future perfect form of the verb in parentheses.

1. (arriver) Quand elle _____, nous pourrons commencer.

2. (finir) Quand il viendra, tu _____.

3. (déjeuner) À deux heures j'_____.

4. (partir) Quand tu téléphoneras, ils _____.

5. (décider) Si vous l'appelez à midi, elle _____.

6. (rentrer) Si tu attends un peu, je _____.

◀ *For more help, see* Future perfect tense, *page 103.*

K Complete each of the following sentences with the pluperfect tense in the if-clause and the conditional perfect tense in the main clause of the verbs in parentheses.

1. Si nous _____ (savoir), nous _____ (venir).

2. Il vous _____ (aider) si vous lui _____ (demander).

3. Elle _____ (ne pas le dire) si elle _____ (être) au courant.

4. Je _____ (ne pas le faire) si on _____ (me dire) que c'était interdit.

5. Si tu _____ (faire) attention, tu _____ (ne pas tomber).

6. S'ils _____ (travailler), ils _____ (réussir) aux examens.

7. Si j'_____ (être) prêt, j'_____ (pouvoir) partir avec eux.

8. Tu _____ (comprendre) si tu _____ (faire) un petit effort.

◀ *For more help, see* Conditional perfect tense, *page 105.*

L Complete each of the following sentences with the present subjunctive or present indicative form of the verb in parentheses.

1. (pouvoir) Il est peu probable qu'il _____ venir.

2. (attendre) Je ne crois pas qu'elle _____ encore.

3. (vouloir) Je sais qu'ils _____ nous accompagner.

4. (savoir) Il est étonnant que tu ne _____ pas la réponse.

5. (être) Je crains qu'il ne _____ pas là.

6. (aller) Nous sommes contents qu'elle _____ en France.

7. (revenir)   Il est certain qu'il _____ demain.

8. (faire)   Il vaut mieux que je _____ ce travail moi-même.

9. (manger)   Maman veut que nous _____ à la maison.

10. (boire)   J'ai apporté de l'eau minérale pour que tu _____ un peu.

11. (prendre)   Je veux que tu _____ un café avec moi.

12. (comprendre)   Nous sommes sûrs qu'elle _____.

13. (venir)   Il est bon que vous _____ avec nous.

14. (rendre)   Il faut que tu t'en _____ compte.

15. (écrire)   Nous viendrons à moins que tu nous _____.

◀ *For more help, see* Subjunctive mood, *pages 111 and 113–114.*

Using your French

Now that you have practiced the mechanics of French, you can use your knowledge to express yourself in meaningful contextual exercises. Each exercise below shows you how to apply one or more grammatical elements in everyday situations. A cross-reference to the relevant grammar points discussed in this book is provided at the end of each exercise. An answer key is provided after the appendices.

A   My dream

Imagine that you are describing a disturbing dream to a friend. To tell what you saw in the dream, use il y avait *("there was/were") plus the elements listed. Add the indefinite article* (un, une, des) *before each noun and make sure the adjectives agree with the nouns.*

MODÈLE   petit/chambre/dans/vieux/maison

     Il y a avait une petite chambre dans une vieille maison.

1. chat/gris/sur/table/rond

_____

2. grand/lit/à côté de/fenêtre/ouvert

_____

3. tableaux/obscur/sur/mur

_____

4. lampe/éteint (*shut*)/près de/fauteuil/défoncé (*battered*)

_____

5. livres/ancien/sous/tapis/usé (*worn, threadbare*)

_____

6. chaussures/déchiré/dans/lavabo/fêlé (*cracked, chipped*)

_____

7. bruit/étrange/derrière/porte/fermé

_____

8. homme/endormi/sur/chaise/cassé

_____

◀ *For more help, see* Introducing determiners, *page 17;* Introducing adjectives, *page 43;* Descriptive adjectives, *page 44;* Introducing prepositions, *page 73.*

B   Moving day

To tell the movers where to put each item they bring into your home, use the imperative mettez *("put") plus the elements listed. Add the definite article* (le, la, l', les) *before each noun and make sure the adjectives agree with the nouns.*

MODÈLE   ordinateur/portable/sur/petit/table

   Mettez l'ordinateur portable sur la petite table.

1. nouveau/imprimante/sur/grand/bureau

_____

2. chaises/autour de/table

_____

3. poste de télé/en face de/canapé/noir

_____

4. fauteuil/blanc/devant/fenêtre/ouvert

_____

5. vêtements/dans/penderie (*closet*)

_____

6. gros/frigo/à côté de/cuisinière (*stove*)

_____

7. assiettes/cassé/dans/poubelle (*trash can, wastebasket*)/vide

_____

8. gros/lampe/à/sous-sol (*basement*)

_____

9. corbeille à papier/derrière/chaise/bleu

_____

10. boîtes/fermé/sous/l'escalier

_____

◀ *For more help, see* Introducing determiners, *page 17;* Introducing adjectives, *page 43;* Descriptive adjectives, *page 44;* Introducing prepositions, *page 73.*

C A scary dream

Émilie describes a scary dream she had last night. To find out what she saw in her dream, combine each group of elements into a sentence in the imperfect tense.

MODÈLE   je/avoir très peur

   J'avais très peur.

1. je/se trouver seule

   _____

2. je/être dans un champ

   _____

3. le ciel/être gris

   _____

4. le vent/souffler

   _____

5. il/commencer à pleuvoir

   _____

6. au loin on/entendre des cris

   _____

7. moi, je/pleurer

   _____

8. la pluie/me/mouiller

   _____

9. je/avoir froid

   _____

10. la terre/trembler

   _____

◀ *For more help, see* Past tenses (imperfect tense), *page 91.*

D   In my apartment building

Alexandre describes what happened in his building today. To find out what happened, combine each group of elements into a sentence in the passé composé. Include the ordinal number to tell which floor the events took place on.

MODÈLE   les Renan/recevoir leurs amis/3

<u>*Au troisième étage les Renan ont reçu leurs amis.*</u>

1. le facteur/apporter un colis pour mon ami Robert/8

   _____

2. Marie Grimbert et son mari/sortir à dix heures/1

   _____

3. une vieille dame/tomber dans le couloir/9

   _____

4. la police/frapper à la porte d'un appartement/4

   _____

5. Monsieur Garric/ne pas aller au travail aujourd'hui/12

   _____

6. le plombier/arriver chez les Doucet/5

   _____

7. Jacquot/sortir les ordures ménagères/6

   _____

8. Mme Hardy/mettre de nouveaux rideaux à sa fenêtre/15

   _____

9. la concierge/nettoyer le tapis/10

   _____

10. des voleurs/entrer dans l'appartement des Mercier/2

   _____

◀ *For more help, see* Passé composé, *pages 97 and 99;* Other limiting adjectives, *page 53.*

E Attitudes and opinions

To tell what people think about the following events, complete each sentence, using the present indicative or present subjunctive in the subordinate clause.

MODÈLE Vous travaillez.

Je ne veux pas ___*que vous travailliez*___.

Nous espérons ___*que vous travaillez*___.

1. Marie-Claire revient.

   a. Je suis content _____.

   b. Nous pensons _____.

   c. Nos amis ne croient pas _____.

   d. Nous sommes sûrs _____.

2. Ils sont ponctuels.

   a. J'espère _____.

   b. Il est important _____.

   c. Il est peu probable _____.

   d. Nous savons _____.

3. Elle répond à tous les messages.

   a. Le chef veut _____.

   b. Il est essentiel _____.

   c. Nous ne pensons pas _____.

   d. Je suis certain _____.

4. Vous savez la réponse.

   a. Il est possible _____.

   b. Je doute _____.

   c. On croit _____.

   d. On espère _____.

5. Tu réussis à vendre ta voiture.

   a. Nous ne pensons pas _____.

   b. Je vois _____.

   c. Il est étonnant _____.

   d. Il paraît _____.

◀ *For more help, see* Subjunctive mood, *pages 111 and 113–114.*

F Expansion

Expand each of the following sentences, using the noun or pronoun in parentheses. Since the subjects of the main and subordinate clauses will be different, you will use the subjunctive.

MODÈLE   Je veux partir. (il)

  Je veux partir et je veux qu'il parte aussi.

1. Je veux dormir. (les enfants)

   _____

2. Je préfère réfléchir. (tu)

   _____

3. Il me faut le faire. (ils)

   _____

4. Il vaut mieux revenir. (elle)

   _____

5. Vous voulez louer une voiture. (nous)

   _____

6. Nous sommes contents de pouvoir partir. (notre ami)

   _____

7. Tu veux sortir. (je)

   _____

8. Nous désirons y aller. (tu)

   _____

9. J'aime mieux être ponctuel. (vous)

   _____

10. Je veux maigrir. (mon copain)

   _____

◀ *For more help, see* Subjunctive mood, *pages 111 and 113.*

G A conversation

Danielle is asking Martine questions about her date with Jean-Claude yesterday. Write the questions Danielle would have asked to elicit Martine's answers, focusing on the italicized phrases and clauses. Use the tu *form and* est-ce que *in your questions.*

MODÈLE   Danielle   *À qui est-ce que tu penses?*

  Martine   Je pense *à Jean-Claude.*

1. Danielle   _____

   Martine   Je suis allée *au café* hier.

2. Danielle   _____

    Martine   J'y suis allée *avec Jean-Claude.*

3. Danielle   _____

    Martine   Il est arrivé *à trois* heures.

4. Danielle   _____

    Martine   J'ai commandé *un café crème.*

5. Danielle   _____

    Martine   *Oui, j'ai mangé une tarte aux poires.*

6. Danielle   _____

    Martine   Nous avons parlé *de notre travail.*

7. Danielle   _____

    Martine   Nous n'avons pas dîné ensemble *parce que j'avais quelque chose à faire.*

8. Danielle   _____

    Martine   Nous comptons nous revoir *demain.*

◀ *For more help, see* Introducing questions, *page 79.*

H   A police investigation

A crime has been committed at the university, and the police are interrogating Caroline Duverger. Write the questions the police would have asked to elicit Caroline's responses, focusing on the italicized phrases and clauses. Use the vous *form and inversion in your questions. For* what? *you may use* que + *inversion or* qu'est-ce que *without inversion.*

MODÈLE   Police   *Comment vous appelez-vous?*

        Caroline   *Je m'appelle Caroline Duverger.*

1. Police   _____

    Caroline   Mon adresse c'est *23 rue de Pascal.*

2. Police   _____

    Caroline   Hier soir *j'étais à la bibliothèque de l'université.*

3. Police   _____

    Caroline   J'y suis allée *parce que j'avais du travail à faire.*

4. Police   _____

    Caroline   Le travail que j'ai fait? *J'ai pris des notes pour mon cours d'histoire.*

5. Police   _____

    Caroline   *Mon ami Philippe Lambert* m'a vu à la bibliothèque.

6. Police   _____

     Caroline   Son numéro de téléphone *c'est le 42 15 61 18.*

7. Police   _____

     Caroline   J'ai quitté la bibliothèque *après avoir fini mon travail.*

8. Police   _____

     Caroline   Après, *je suis allée voir mon amie Françoise.*

◀ For more help, see Introducing questions, *page 79.*

I   Summer plans

Some friends are discussing their summer plans. To tell what each person wants or plans to do, combine each group of elements into a sentence in the present tense. In each case, you will determine which preposition, if any, is used before the infinitive.

MODÈLE   Gabrielle/décider/suivre des cours

     Gabrielle décide de suivre des cours.

1. Marc/vouloir/apprendre/parler japonais

_____

2. Louise et Léa/essayer/trouver un travail

_____

3. Paul et Pierre/s'intéresser/voyager en Europe

_____

4. ils/commencer/chercher des billets d'avion

_____

5. Jacqueline/préférer/rester à la maison

_____

6. Arthur/venir/trouver un nouvel appartement

_____

7. Les Gagnon/inviter Géraldine/passer l'été dans leur chalet de montagne.

_____

_____

8. Mathilde/suggérer à ses amis/aider les pauvres

_____

◀ For more help, see Present tense, *pages 87 and 89;* Introducing prepositions, *pages 73–74.*

J Backgrounds and events

To tell what happened at the office, combine each group of elements into a sentence, using quand *to connect the clauses. The verb expressing background action will be in the imperfect tense, while the passé composé will be used to label the event. Note that weather, the time, and feelings are usually background actions, not events, in past time.*

MODÈLE   faire soleil/Antoine/ouvrir sa porte

    Il faisait soleil quand Antoine a ouvert sa porte.

1. être neuf heures quinze/il/sortir

2. faire beau/Amélie/arriver au bureau

3. être tard/la secrétaire/venir

4. faire froid dans le bureau/les employés/commencer à travailler

5. être midi et demi/je/descendre déjeuner

6. je/manger/commencer à pleuvoir

7. être tout mouillé/je/retourner au bureau

8. les rues être sèches/je/quitter le bureau

◀ *For more help, see* Passé composé, *pages 97 and 99;* Past tenses (imperfect tense), *page 91.*

K Oui et non

To tell what doesn't happen in contrast to what does happen, write a complete sentence, using the phrase in parentheses and the correct indirect object pronoun.

MODÈLE   Je prête mon vélo à mon ami Charles. (ma voiture)

    Je ne lui prête pas ma voiture.

1. Nous montrons nos photos à notre chef. (nos courriels)

2. J'ai envoyé les données au directeur. (les documents)

3. Elle a dit son adresse à l'agent de police. (son numéro de téléphone)

_____

4. Les conseillers ont rendu les dossiers à la secrétaire. (l'argent)

_____

5. Marc a offert un collier à sa fiancée. (une montre)

_____

6. Le médecin donne les ordonnances à ses patients. (les médicaments)

_____

7. L'oncle à laissé son argent à ses neveux. (son entreprise)

_____

8. Il a vendu sa maison à ses voisins. (toute sa propriété)

_____

◀ _For more help, see_ Personal pronouns, _page 25;_ Introducing adverbs, _page 59._

L I don't know

Answer the following questions, saying that you don't know whether the things asked about are true or not. Use the pronoun y or en in each of your answers.

MODÈLES Est-ce que Luc a des documents?

  Je ne sais pas s'il en a.

Est-ce que Luc travaille dans ce quartier?

  Je ne sais pas s'il y travaille.

1. Est-ce que notre bureau achète des logiciels?

_____

2. Est-ce que notre chef passe ses vacances à Paris?

_____

3. Est-ce que le programmeur travaille chez lui?

_____

4. Est-ce que la secrétaire envoie des messages?

_____

5. Est-ce que les conseillers sont dans la salle de conférence?

_____

6. Est-ce que nous avons signé des contrats?

_____

7. Est-ce que notre bureau a embauché (*hired*) de nouveaux employés?

_____

8. Est-ce que nous allons organiser un dîner d'affaires au restaurant du coin?

_____

◀ *For more help, see* Personal pronouns, *page 25.*

M Problems and solutions

State a solution to each of the following problems, using the elements in parentheses plus a double object pronoun.

MODÈLE   Paul ne sait pas le numéro de téléphone de Julien. (je/aller/dire)

___*Je vais le lui dire.*___

1. Le petit garçon ne sait pas lire ce livre. (il faut/lire)

_____

2. Ces enfants n'ont pas de livres en français. (nous/devoir/acheter)

_____

3. Ces parents ne donnent pas de conseils à leurs enfants. (ils/devoir/donner)

_____

4. Nos cousins veulent voir le musée. (nous/aller/emmener)

_____

5. Emma et moi, nous voulons du parfum français. (Marguerite/pouvoir/rapporter de France)

_____

6. Julien a besoin de ces livres. (je/compter/prêter)

_____

7. Camille aime recevoir des cartes postales. (on/devoir/envoyer)

_____

8. Alexandre voudrait du café. (je/aller/préparer)

_____

◀ *For more help, see* Personal pronouns, *page 25.*

N   Louis can't find anything!

Create dialogues between Louis and Micheline about all the items Louis can't find in the office. In each dialogue, use the correct object pronoun and pay attention to the position of the pronouns. Louis and Micheline use the tu *form with each other.*

MODÈLE   Où sont les documents?

Louis   *Je ne les trouve pas.*

Micheline   *Cherche-les. Tu les trouveras.*

1. Où est ma serviette? (*briefcase*)

   Louis   _____

   Micheline   _____

2. Où est le cédé?

   Louis   _____

   Micheline   _____

3. Où est l'agrafeuse? (*stapler*)

   Louis   _____

   Micheline   _____

4. Où sont les nouveaux logiciels?

   Louis   _____

   Micheline   _____

5. Où est la liste des nouveaux employés?

   Louis   _____

   Micheline   _____

6. Où sont les dossiers?

   Louis   _____

   Micheline   _____

7. Où est mon ordinateur portable?

   Louis   _____

   Micheline   _____

8. Où sont mes clés USB?

   Louis   _____

   Micheline   _____

◀ *For more help, see* Personal pronouns, *page 25.*

O Voyages

To explain the following situations, combine each group of elements into a complete sentence. You will have to select the correct preposition, if any, that connects the verb to the infinitive, as well as the correct preposition for each geographical name.

MODÈLE   Margot/se décider/trouver un appartement/Paris

Margot se décide à trouver un appartement à Paris.

1. Julie/vouloir/travailler/France

2. Samuel/préférer/rester/États-Unis

3. mes cousins/refuser/aller/Espagne

4. Mathieu/continuer/faire ses études/la Nouvelle-Orléans

5. Pauline et son mari/chercher/trouver un logement/Mexique

6. Camille/réussir/trouver un poste/Londres

7. Les Duhamel/aimer/passer l'hiver/Floride

8. Isaac et moi/venir/arriver/Le Havre

◀ *For more help, see* Introducing prepositions, *pages 73–74.*

P Combining sentences

Combine each pair of sentences into a single sentence, using the conjunction in parentheses. Use the present subjunctive tense in the subordinate clause.

MODÈLE   Je le lui ai dit. Il le sait. (pour que)

Je le lui ai dit pour qu'il le sache.

1. J'irai au cinéma. Tu ne peux pas m'accompagner. (à moins que)

2. J'expliquerai tout encore une fois. Tu comprends. (pour que)

3. Nous sortirons. Il ne fait pas beau. (bien que)

_____

4. On partira. Elle revient. (avant que)

_____

5. Je resterai avec l'enfant. Il s'endort. (jusqu'à ce que)

_____

6. Nous réussirons à le faire. Nous nous mettons à travailler. (pourvu que)

_____

7. Cet employé travaille peu. Son chef s'en rend compte. (sans que)

_____

8. Je n'y vais pas. Il n'est pas là. (de peur que)

_____

◀ *For more help, see* Introducing conjunctions, *page 65;* Subjunctive mood, *pages 111 and 113–114.*

Q This evening

Sylvie is telling what this evening at home will be like. To find out what she is saying, combine each group of elements into a complete sentence in the future tense.

MODÈLE   ma famille/passer la soirée à la maison

Ma famille passera la soirée à la maison.

1. ma mère/faire le dîner

_____

2. ma sœur et moi, nous/laver et sécher la vaisselle

_____

3. mon frère/regarder un match à la télé

_____

4. mon père/lire le journal

_____

5. mes grands-parents/jouer aux cartes

_____

6. ma cousine/venir nous voir

_____

7. les voisins/prendre le dessert avec nous

_____

8. ma tante/voir un film

_____

9. moi, je/être contente de parler avec tout le monde

_____

10. nous/pouvoir s'amuser ensemble

_____

◀ *For more help, see* Future tense, *page 93.*

R Winning the lottery

To tell what the following people would do if they won the lottery, combine each group of elements into a complete sentence in the conditional tense.

MODÈLE Jean-Paul/ne travailler plus

   Jean-Paul ne travaillerait plus.

1. Justine/monter une affaire

_____

2. mes voisins/prendre la retraite

_____

3. Claude/faire un voyage en Asie

_____

4. moi/acheter une maison à Tahiti

_____

5. mes grands-parents/être contents

_____

6. toi/aller habiter au bord de la mer

_____

7. nous/vouloir aider notre famille

_____

8. moi/pouvoir acheter une Lamborghini

_____

9. Philippe/payer ses dettes

_____

10. on/dîner dans les meilleurs restaurants

_____

◀ *For more help, see* Conditional tense, *page 95.*

S Never, never, never

To tell what the following people will not do, combine each group of elements into a complete sentence in the future tense.

MODÈLE   je/ne pas/changer de travail

   Je ne changerai pas de travail.

1. Lucie/ne jamais/sortir avec Mathieu

   _____

2. mon oncle et ma tante/ne pas/revenir de France cette année

   _____

   _____

3. toi/ne plus/prêter de l'argent à Michel

   _____

4. nous/ne rien/recevoir pour notre anniversaire

   _____

5. vous/ne personne/voir au bureau

   _____

6. je/ne plus/faire les courses le matin

   _____

7. Émile et Jacqueline/ne jamais plus/aller en vacances ensemble

   _____

   _____

8. personne/ne/compléter le projet aujourd'hui

   _____

9. nous/ne jamais/savoir ce qui est arrivé

   _____

10. je/ne plus/être dans le même rayon que toi

   _____

◀ *For more help, see* Future tense, *page 93;* Introducing adverbs, *page 59.*

T It could be otherwise

To tell what has to change for a business meeting to be successful, combine each pair of sentences into a conditional sentence. Each sentence will consist of a main clause in the conditional and an if-clause in the imperfect.

MODÈLE   La réunion commence à huit heures du matin. Tout le monde ne peut pas venir.

Si la réunion ne commençait pas à huit heures du matin,

tout le monde pourrait venir.

1. On n'a pas préparé l'ordre du jour (*agenda*). On perd tant de temps.

2. Tout le monde parle pendant la réunion. On n'avance pas assez vite.

3. On n'a pas toutes les données (*data*). On ne peut pas proposer les solutions nécessaires.

4. Notre directeur ne parle pas clairement. Les employés ne comprennent pas les problèmes.

5. L'entreprise ne sert pas le déjeuner. Il faut interrompre la réunion.

6. Les employés n'ont pas les documents. Ils ne sont pas préparés.

7. Nous n'avons pas les comptes-rendus. Nous ne savons pas combien on a vendu.

8. La réunion n'est pas bien organisée. Il nous faut rester jusqu'à neuf heures du soir.

◀ *For more help, see* Conditional tense, *page 95;* Conditional perfect tense, *page 105.*

U   A better vacation

To tell what should have happened for the following people to have a great vacation, combine each pair of sentences into a conditional sentence. Each sentence will consist of an if-clause in the past perfect (pluperfect) tense and a main clause in the conditional perfect.

MODÈLE   On est partis au mois d'août. Il a fait si chaud.

   Si on n'était pas partis au mois d'août, il n'aurait pas fait

   si chaud.

1. Nous sommes allés à la plage. Nous ne nous sommes pas amusés.

  _____

  _____

2. L'hôtel n'était pas propre. On se sentait mal a l'aise.

  _____

  _____

3. Les restaurants étaient mauvais. Je suis tombé malade.

  _____

  _____

4. Il a plu tous les jours. On n'a pas pu nager.

  _____

  _____

5. Le cinéma était fermé. On n'a pas vu des films.

  _____

  _____

6. J'ai oublié mon livre. Je n'ai pas pu lire.

  _____

  _____

7. Nos amis ne sont pas venus avec nous. Les vacances étaient désagréables.

  _____

  _____

8. Nous y sommes restés trop longtemps. On s'est ennuyés.

  _____

  _____

◀ *For more help, see* Conditional tense, *page 95;* Past perfect (pluperfect) tense, *page 101;* Conditional perfect tense, *page 105.*

V Growing our business

To tell what is needed to grow the business, combine each pair of sentences into a single sentence. Use the subjunctive in the subordinate clause.

MODÈLE   Nous avons besoin d'une secrétaire. Elle doit être bilingue.

Nous avons besoin d'une secrétaire qui soit bilingue.

1. Nous cherchons un chef de bureau. Il doit connaître la bureautique.

   _____

2. On voudrait trouver un secrétaire. Elle doit savoir écrire en allemand et en anglais.

   _____

   _____

3. Il nous faut des représentants. Ils doivent pouvoir voyager souvent.

   _____

4. Nous avons besoin d'une banque. Elle doit avoir des succursales en Asie.

   _____

5. Je cherche un directeur. Il doit comprendre les nouvelles technologies.

   _____

6. Il nous faut un fournisseur. Il doit garantir la sécurité de notre réseau (*network*).

   _____

   _____

7. Nous voulons embaucher des employés. Ils doivent faire un bon travail.

   _____

   _____

8. Nous cherchons de nouveaux marchés. Ils doivent être rentables (*profitable*).

   _____

   _____

◀ *For more help, see* Subjunctive mood, *pages 111 and 113–114.*

W Un peu de réalisme

Marceline tries to bring her friend Lisette back to reality by telling her that her ideas about their friends are not realistic. Respond to Lisette's assertions, using the correct negative words.

MODÈLE   Lisette   Jean-Luc connaît quelqu'un à Marseille.

Marceline   *Non, Jean-Luc ne connaît personne à Marseille.*

1. Lisette   Quelqu'un va donner un travail à Emma.

   Marceline   _____

2. Lisette   Philippe a toujours beaucoup à faire.

      Marceline   _____

3. Lisette   Jacques a souvent de très bonnes notes.

      Marceline   _____

4. Lisette   Léonie trouve quelque chose d'intéressant.

      Marceline   _____

5. Lisette   Juliette achète une Ferrari ou une Lamborghini.

      Marceline   _____

6. Lisette   Florian parle avec quelqu'un en ce moment.

      Marceline   _____

7. Lisette   Stella est encore à la campagne.

      Marceline   _____

8. Lisette   Matthieu est déjà arrivé.

      Marceline   _____

◀ *For more help, see* Introducing adverbs, *page 59.*

X   It had already happened

To explain what had already happened when certain events occurred, combine each group of elements into a complete sentence. Use the passé composé in the first clause and déjà *plus the pluperfect (past perfect) tense in the second.*

MODÈLE   Julien/rentrer : nous/sortir

     Quand Julien est rentré, nous étions déjà sortis.

1. nous/arriver à l'aéroport : l'avion/partir

     _____

2. Luc/se lever : nous/servir le petit déjeuner

     _____

3. Lucie/envoyer sa demande d'emploi : l'entreprise/embaucher quelqu'un

     _____

     _____

4. Maurice/laisser le pourboire : Pierre/payer l'addition

     _____

5. les invités/frapper à la porte : Monique/s'habiller

     _____

6. le taxi/arriver : Christine et son mari/faire leurs valises

     _____

7. le chef/m'appeler : je/finir mon travail

_____

8. les employés/venir : on/fermer le bureau

_____

◀ *For more help, see* Passé composé, *pages 97 and 99;* Past perfect (pluperfect) tense, *page 101.*

Y   Organizing a trip

To tell how a trip was organized, combine each group of elements into a complete sentence in the passé composé, using the passive voice.

MODÈLE   le voyage/organiser/le chef de bureau

   Le voyage a été organisé par le chef de bureau.

1. tous les employés/inviter

_____

2. les billets de train/acheter/la secrétaire

_____

3. les réservations/faire/le chef de bureau

_____

4. l'itinéraire/décider/les employés

_____

5. un guide/embaucher/une agence de voyage

_____

6. des activités/organiser/par l'hôtel

_____

7. des rencontres professionnelles/arranger/l'entreprise

_____

8. des visites intéressantes/programmer

_____

◀ *For more help, see* Passive voice, *page 107.*

Z Making choices

Create a dialogue, using each group of elements. Use the correct forms of the interrogative adjective quel *and the demonstrative pronoun* celui.

MODÈLES cours/suivre/le professeur Martel

——*Quel cours suivez-vous?*——

——*Celui du professeur Martel.*——

train/prendre/(il) part pour Lille

——*Quel train prenez-vous?*——

——*Celui qui part pour Lille.*——

1. gants/acheter/(ils) sont en solde

_____

_____

2. documents/lire/(ils) étaient sur mon bureau

_____

_____

3. voiture/préférer/mon oncle

_____

_____

4. villes/visiter/(elles) sont présentées sur mon itinéraire

_____

_____

5. maison/vendre/notre quartier

_____

_____

6. employés/embaucher/(ils) parlent au moins deux langues étrangères

_____

_____

7. livres/emprunter/mes amis

_____

_____

8. tableaux/vouloir regarder/(ils) sont dans le musée d'art

_____

_____

◀ *For more help, see* Demonstrative pronouns, *page 37;* Interrogative pronouns, *pages 39–40.*

AA   Touring in France

To compare what you are seeing with what you have seen before, create a dialogue from each group of elements. Use demonstrative adjectives, the comparative, and the superlative.

MODÈLE   place/grand/ville

—Est-ce que cette place est plus grande que l'autre?

—Oui, c'est la place la plus grande de la ville.

1. église/ancien/ville

2. magasin/cher/quartier

3. restaurant/bon/rue

4. industries/important/région

5. écoles/connu/pays

6. paysage/admiré/province

7. fleuve/large/Midi

8. ports/actif/continent

◄ *For more help, see* Demonstrative adjectives, *page 49;* Comparison of adjectives, *page 47.*

BB How things are done

To tell how people perform actions, combine each pair of sentences into a single sentence, using an adverb.

MODÈLE Maurice s'exprime. C'est facile.

   Maurice s'exprime facilement.

1. Le vieil homme marche. Il est lent.

   _____

2. Chloé participe à la création du site Web. Elle est active.

   _____

3. Noah répond. Il est vif.

   _____

4. Le jeune couple vit. Ils sont heureux.

   _____

5. Tout le monde se promène. C'est agréable.

   _____

6. Je me lève. Je suis rapide.

   _____

7. Léa sort. Elle est furieuse.

   _____

8. Les enfants chantent. Leurs voix sont douces.

   _____

◀ *For more help, see* Introducing adverbs, *page 57.*

CC Yesterday was a busy day

To tell all the things that happened yesterday, combine each group of elements into a complete sentence in the passé composé. Write out all numbers in your answers.

MODÈLE nos amis/nous téléphoner 10 fois

   Nos amis nous ont téléphoné dix fois.

1. Pierre et Lucie/revenir d'Europe à 9 heures

   _____

2. je/répondre à 45 courriels

   _____

3. Émile/dépenser 800 euros au grand magasin

   _____

4. Ma tante Adèle/gagner 15.000 euros à la loterie

_____

5. Sophie/lire 260 pages

_____

6. Robert/parler 50 minutes au téléphone

_____

7. le restaurant du coin/servir 370 clients

_____

8. nous/connaître des touristes de 21 pays différents

_____

◀ _For more help, see_ Passé composé, _pages 97 and 99;_ Cardinal numbers, _page 173._

DD Attitudes and feelings

To tell what people think, combine each pair of sentences into a single sentence, using either an infinitive or a subordinate clause in the subjunctive.

MODÈLES Je suis content. Je suis à Paris.

Je suis content d'être à Paris.

Je suis content. Vous êtes à Paris.

Je suis content que vous soyez à Paris.

1. Ils doutent. Nous pouvons les aider.

_____

2. Nous sommes sûrs. Nous pouvons les aider.

_____

3. Je ne crois pas. Vous acceptez l'offre d'emploi.

_____

4. Vous voulez. Vous acceptez l'offre d'emploi.

_____

5. J'ai peur. Il est en retard.

_____

6. Il a peur. Il est en retard.

_____

7. Elle est ravi. Tu viens.

_____

8. Tu es content. Tu viens.

_____

◄ *For more help, see* Subjunctive mood, *pages 111 and 113–114.*

EE No, they're the same

Louise and Hélène are comparing people and things. Louise says that someone or something is more _____ than someone or something else. Hélène disagrees, suggesting that they are equally _____. Combine each group of elements into a complete sentence by Louise, which Hélène contradicts. Make sure that adjectives agree with the nouns they modify.

MODÈLE   Jacques/amusant/Rémy

Louise   _Jacques est plus amusant que Rémy._

Hélène   _Pas vrai. Rémy est aussi amusant que Jacques._

1. notre ville/élégant/Paris

Louise _____

Hélène _____

2. Philippe/intelligent/Marc

Louise _____

Hélène _____

3. ce roman/passionnant/l'autre roman

Louise _____

Hélène _____

4. cette chanteuse française/célèbre/la chanteuse canadienne

Louise _____

Hélène _____

5. cette tarte au citron/bon/la tarte aux poires

Louise _____

Hélène _____

6. cet appartement/cher/cette maison

Louise _____

Hélène _____

7. Élisabeth/charmant/Inès

Louise _____

Hélène _____

8. cette étudiante/gentil/le professeur

Louise _____

Hélène _____

◀ *For more help, see* Comparison of adjectives, *page 47.*

FF Antoine and his family

To tell how Antoine and his family get ready for the day, combine each group of elements into a complete sentence in the present tense.

MODÈLE   Antoine/se lever/6h

    Antoine se lève à six heures.

1. il/se brosser les dents

_____

2. sa sœur Camille/se réveiller/7h

_____

3. Antoine/se raser/et prendre une douche

_____

4. sa mère/se laver/la tête

_____

5. tout le monde/s'habiller/vite

_____

6. ils/se préparer/pour la journée

_____

7. Antoine et Camille/s'asseoir/pour le petit déjeuner

_____

8. ils/se dire/au revoir

_____

◀ *For more help, see* Reflexive/reciprocal pronouns, *page 29;* Present tense, *pages 87 and 89.*

GG L'employé idéal

To describe the kind of employee a firm wishes to hire, write a job advertisement, using each of the following phrases. Use the vous *form of the reflexive verb in the present tense.*

MODÈLE   ne pas se plaindre du travail

    Vous ne vous plaignez pas du travail.

1. s'intéresser aux projets

_____

2. ne pas s'énerver facilement

_____

3. se passionner pour les idées

_____

4. ne pas se fâcher avec les collègues

_____

5. s'adresser poliment à tout le monde

_____

6. se soucier de la qualité du travail

_____

7. se donner la peine d'apprendre des nouvelles technologies

_____

8. ne pas s'en aller du bureau avant cinq heures

_____

◀ For more help, see Reflexive/reciprocal pronouns, page 29.

HH   Discussing the day's news

Create a dialogue about what happened yesterday, using each group of elements. The first person in the dialogue tells what happened, and the second one asks a question about it, using est-ce que. _Use the passé composé in each dialogue. In each question, replace the direct object noun of the statement with its corresponding pronoun. Make the past participle agree where necessary._

MODÈLE   Claudette/trouver/le document/quand

1   —Claudette a trouvé le document.
    —Quand est-ce qu'elle l'a trouvé?

1. les enfants/ne pas faire/leurs devoirs/pourquoi

_____

_____

2. mes parents/acheter/une nouvelle voiture/où

_____

_____

3. je/recevoir/deux messages mystérieux/à quelle heure

_____

_____

4. je/perdre/mes clés/quand

_____

_____

5. nous/regarder/les actualités/avec qui

_____

_____

6. Paul/retrouver/Agathe et Eugénie/où

_____

_____

7. les Garnier/vendre/leur maison/à qui

_____

_____

8. Aurélie/voir/le nouveau film italien/avec qui

_____

_____

◀ *For more help, see* Passé composé, *pages 97 and 99*; Personal pronouns, *pages 23, 25, and 27*; Introducing questions, *page 79.*

Pronoun review

Personal pronouns

Always used with a verb				May be used alone
	OBJECT			
SUBJECT	**DIRECT**	**REFLEXIVE**	**INDIRECT**	**DISJUNCTIVE**
je	*me*	*me*	*me*	*moi*
tu	*te*	*te*	*te*	*toi*
il, elle, on	*le, la, l'*	*se*	*lui*	*lui, elle, soi*
nous	*nous*	*nous*	*nous*	*nous*
vous	*vous*	*vous*	*vous*	*vous*
ils, elles	*les*	*se*	*leur*	*eux, elles*

Comparison of relative and interrogative pronouns

RELATIVE PRONOUNS

	PERSON	THING	INDEFINITE
SUBJECT	*qui* (or form of *lequel*)	*qui* (or form of *lequel*)	*ce qui*
OBJECT	*que*	*que* (or form of *lequel*)	*ce que*
OBJECT OF *de*	*de qui* (or *dont*)	*dont* (or form of *duquel*)	*ce dont*
OBJECT OF ANY OTHER PREPOSITION	preposition + *qui* (or form of *lequel*)	preposition + form of *lequel où* (for time or place)	*ce* + preposition + *quoi*

INTERROGATIVE PRONOUNS (SHORT FORM)

	PERSON	THING
SUBJECT	*qui*	—
OBJECT	*qui*	*que*
OBJECT OF A PREPOSITION	preposition + *qui*	preposition + *quoi*

INTERROGATIVE PRONOUNS (LONG FORM)

Interrogative pronoun + *est-ce* + relative pronoun

	PERSON	THING
SUBJECT	*qui est-ce qui*	*qu'est-ce qui*
OBJECT	*qui est-ce que*	*qu'est-ce que*

Adjectives and pronouns

DEMONSTRATIVE ADJECTIVES AND PRONOUNS

	ADJECTIVES (USED WITH A NOUN)	PRONOUNS (USED WITHOUT A NOUN)
MASCULINE SINGULAR	*ce livre (-ci, -là)*	*celui (-ci, -là, or a prepositional phrase)*
MASCULINE SINGULAR BEFORE A VOWEL OR SILENT h	*cet homme*	*celui*
FEMININE SINGULAR	*cette dame*	*celle*
MASCULINE PLURAL	*ces étudiants*	*ceux*
FEMININE PLURAL	*ces étudiantes*	*celles*

INTERROGATIVE ADJECTIVES AND PRONOUNS

	ADJECTIVES (USED WITH A NOUN)	PRONOUNS (USED WITHOUT A NOUN)
MASCULINE SINGULAR	*quel livre?*	*lequel?*
FEMININE SINGULAR	*quelle dame?*	*laquelle?*
MASCULINE PLURAL	*quels étudiants?*	*lesquels?*
FEMININE PLURAL	*quelles filles?*	*lesquelles?*

The four forms of *lequel* are also used as relative pronouns (see page 33).

Determiners: A summary

Normally, only one determiner is used before a noun.

DETERMINERS FOR WORDS BEGINNING WITH A CONSONANT OR VOICED *h*

MASCULINE SINGULAR	FEMININE SINGULAR	PLURAL
un café, un héros	*une glace, une haine*	*des livres, des tables, des héros*
le café	*la glace*	*les livres, les tables*
mon café, ton café, etc.	*ma glace, ta glace,* etc.	*mes livres, tes livres,* etc.
ce café	*cette glace*	*ces livres, ces tables*
quel café	*quelle glace*	*quels livres, quelles tables*
quelque café	*quelque glace*	*quelques livres, quelques tables*
du café, du homard	*de la glace*	*des livres, des tables, des homards*

DETERMINERS FOR WORDS BEGINNING WITH A VOWEL OR SILENT *h*

MASCULINE SINGULAR	FEMININE SINGULAR	PLURAL
un amour	*une eau*	Plural forms are the same as the plural forms in the preceding chart.
l'amour, l'hôtel	*l'eau*	
mon amour, ton amour, etc.	*mon eau, ton eau,* etc.	
cet amour	*cette eau*	
quel amour	*quelle eau*	
de l'amour	*de l'eau*	

A determiner is not needed

1. after some prepositions (as in *sans doute*).

2. with a noun of nationality, profession, or religion (as in *Il est américain.*).

3. when one noun is used to describe another (as in *un professeur d'art, une fête de famille*).

4. in expressing possession (as in *l'ami d'Henri*).

5. in a partitive construction under special circumstances (see page 17).

APPENDIX C
Patterns of irregular verbs

PATTERN I   L-shaped verbs

These verbs show a spelling change, including accents, in the singular and third-person plural forms.

> *mener, acheter, geler, jeter, appeler, payer, envoyer, ennuyer, mourir, mouvoir, pouvoir, vouloir, venir, revenir, devenir, prévenir, tenir, retenir*

PATTERN II   Box verbs with regular singular forms

> *faire, taire, plaire,* traire, voir,† croire, boire, haïr,† vêtir, fuir, cuire, nuire, écrire, suffire, rire, courir, prendre, comprendre, apprendre, surprendre, pendre, coudre, moudre*

PATTERN III   Box verbs with regular plural forms

> *battre, mettre, permettre, promettre, soumettre, servir, partir, mentir, sortir, dormir, sentir, savoir, vêtir, valoir, suivre, vivre*

PATTERN IV   Mistaken-identity verbs

These are *-ir* verbs that take *-er* endings.

> *offrir, souffrir, ouvrir, couvrir, découvrir, cueillir, accueillir, recueillir*

PATTERN V   Disappearing-letter verbs

If the infinitive ending of one of these verbs is dropped, the final consonant sound is silent. Since the final consonant has no sound, it is not written in the verb's singular forms.

> *naître,* connaître,* paître,* croître,* accroître,* craindre, plaindre, atteindre, éteindre, peindre, joindre, résoudre, partir, sortir, mentir, dormir, sentir, servir, suivre, vivre, mettre, battre, pleuvoir*

PATTERN VI   Soft-consonant verbs

These include *-ger* verbs, which add *-e* after the *g* when the verb ending begins with any letter other than *e* or *i*, and *-cer* verbs, which place a cedilla under the *c* (*ç*) under the same circumstances.

> *manger, commencer, placer*

PATTERN VII   Change-under-stress verbs

These include *-evoir* verbs that are regular in the *nous/vous* forms, but change the *e* of the stem to *oi* when the stress is on the stem (see Pattern I) and eliminate the *v* in the singular forms (see Pattern V).

> *devoir, recevoir, percevoir, s'apercevoir*

---

* With the third-person singular ending *-ît*.
† With the infinitive ending *-r*.

Verbs whose infinitives end in *-aître*, *-oître*, *-indre*, *-yer* (except *-eyer* verbs), and *-evoir* follow the same patterns within their groups.

> *connaître, craindre, essayer, devoir*

Some irregular verbs have patterns all their own.

> *avoir, être, aller, falloir, vaincre* (regular in sound, since *c* and *qu* have the same sound), *bouillir, s'asseoir*

avoir	*être*	*aller*	*falloir*
j'ai	*je suis*	*je vais*	
tu as	*tu es*	*tu vas*	
il/elle a	*il/elle est*	*il/elle va*	*il faut*
nous avons	*nous sommes*	*nous allons*	
vous avez	*vous êtes*	*vous allez*	
ils/elles ont	*ils/elles sont*	*ils/elles vont*	

APPENDIX D

Literary tenses

A few verb tenses not mentioned in the text are encountered only in reading. It is not necessary to learn these tenses now, but it is important to be able to recognize them. As literary tenses, they are never used in conversation or informal writing—only in formal writing (for example, literature, scholarship, and formal speeches).

Passé simple and passé antérieur

These tenses are the literary equivalents of the passé composé and the pluperfect, respectively. They are translated in the same way, but using them gives a special formal tone to the writing and shows seriousness of purpose. Remember that it is enough to be able to recognize them.

PASSÉ SIMPLE

parler (-er VERBS)	finir (-ir AND -re VERBS)	connaître (-re AND -oir VERBS)	avoir
je parlai	je finis	je connus	j'eus
tu parlas	tu finis	tu connus	tu eus
il/elle parla	il/elle finit	il/elle connut	il/elle eut
nous parlâmes	nous finîmes	nous connûmes	nous eûmes
vous parlâtes	vous finîtes	vous connûtes	vous eûtes
ils/elles parlèrent	ils/elles finirent	ils/elles connurent	ils/elles eurent

Verbs with irregular stems in the passé simple include the following. Note that the past participle often serves as the stem of the passé simple.

s'asseoir → je m'assis	être → je fus	recevoir → je reçus
craindre → je craignis	courir → je courus	savoir → je sus
écrire → j'écrivis	croire → je crus	se taire → je me tus
joindre → je joignis	devoir → je dus	valoir → je valus
faire → je fis	falloir → il fallut	vivre → je vécus
mettre → je mis	lire → je lus	vouloir → je voulus
naître → je naquis	plaire → je plus	venir → je vins
prendre → je pris	pleuvoir → il plut	tenir → je tins
voir → je vis	pouvoir → je pus	

There are three groups of endings for the passé simple, and all verbs use one of these groups. This means that all passé simple forms can be derived from the first- or third-person singular form of an irregular verb, since the endings are the same as those of regular verbs.

Notice that irregular passé simple stems often resemble either the past participle (for example, connaître → connu → je connus) or the alternative stem in the present—the one used for the nous and vous forms if they are different (for example, écrire → nous écrivons → j'écrivis).

For some very irregular stems, the ancient Romans must take responsibility. For instance, for the verb être, the passé simple je fus comes from the Latin simple past of "to be": fui.

Once the passé simple of *être* and *avoir* is learned, the passé antérieur is easy: It uses the passé simple of the auxiliary verb plus the past participle of the main verb. Otherwise, it follows all of the rules that you learned for the passé composé.

parler	finir	connaître	être
j'eus parlé	j'eus fini	j'eus connu	j'eus été
tu eus parlé	tu eus fini	tu eus connu	tu eus été
etc.	etc.	etc.	etc.

A verb that uses *être* as its auxiliary in the passé composé does so here too (for example, *elle fut allée, nous vous fûmes levés*).

Imperfect subjunctive and pluperfect subjunctive

These literary tenses are easy to recognize because of the *-ss-* in most of the endings.

The imperfect subjunctive is formed from the same stem as the passé simple, so once the irregular stems for the passé simple can be recognized, so will those for the imperfect subjunctive. The pluperfect subjunctive uses the imperfect subjunctive of the auxiliary verb plus the past participle of the main verb. All other rules are the same as those for the perfect tenses.

In summary, once the stems and endings for the passé simple are known, recognition of the other three literary tenses is easy.

IMPERFECT SUBJUNCTIVE

parler	finir	connaître	être
que je parlasse	que je finisse	que je connusse	que je fusse
que tu parlasses	que tu finisses	que tu connusses	que tu fusses
qu'il parlât	qu'il finît	qu'il connût	qu'il fût
que nous parlassions	que nous finissions	que nous connussions	que nous fussions
que vous parlassiez	que vous finissiez	que vous connussiez	que vous fussiez
qu'ils parlassent	qu'ils finissent	qu'ils connussent	qu'ils fussent

PLUPERFECT SUBJUNCTIVE

parler	finir	connaître	être
que j'eusse parlé	que j'eusse fini	que j'eusse connu	que j'eusse été
que tu eusses parlé	que tu eusses fini	que tu eusses connu	que tu eusses été
etc.	etc.	etc.	etc.

A verb that uses *être* as its auxiliary in the passé composé does so here too (for example, *qu'elle fût allée, que nous nous fussions levés*).

Compound tenses

Être special group*

In this group, *être* is the auxiliary and the past participle agrees with the subject.

SUBJECT	(*ne*)	(OBJECT)	AUXILIARY	(*pas*)	(ADVERB)	PAST PARTICIPLE	
je	ne	y	suis	pas	souvent	*arrivé(e)(s)*	*resté(e)(s)*
tu	n'	en	es		vite	*tombé(e)(s)*	*descendu(e)(s)*
il/elle			est		etc.	*allé(e)(s)*	*mort(e)(s)*
nous			sommes			*entré(e)(s)*	*venu(e)(s)*
vous			êtes			*parti(e)(s)*	*né(e)(s)*
ils/elles			sont			*sorti(e)(s)*	

Reflexive/reciprocal verbs

In this group, *être* is the auxiliary and the past participle agrees with the preceding direct object.

SUBJECT	(*ne*)	(OBJECT)	AUXILIARY	(*pas*)	(ADVERB)	PAST PARTICIPLE
je	ne	me	suis	pas	bien	*amusé(e)(s)*
tu		t'	es		encore	*levé(e)(s)*
il/elle		s'	est		etc.	*reposé(e)(s)*
nous		nous	sommes			*habillé(e)(s)*
vous		vous	êtes			*réveillé(e)(s)*
ils/elles		se	sont			*lavé les mains†*

---

* See page 97 for a list of verbs that commonly take *être* as their auxiliary.

† In this case, *les mains* is the direct object of the verb; since it does not precede the verb, there is no agreement.

All other verbs

In this group, *avoir* is the auxiliary and the past participle agrees with the preceding direct object.

SUBJECT	(*ne*)	(OBJECT)	AUXILIARY	(*pas*)	(ADVERB)	PAST PARTICIPLE
je	*ne*	*les*	*ai*	*pas*	*beaucoup*	REGULAR VERBS
tu		*m'en*	*as*		*déjà*	*parlé*
il/elle		*nous les*	*a*		*encore*	*montré(e)(s)*
nous		*vous en*	*avons*		*assez*	*donné(e)(s)*
vous		*les lui*	*avez*		*toujours*	*répondu*
ils/elles	*n'*	*y*	*ont*		*bien*	*sorti(e)(s)*
					etc.	etc.
						IRREGULAR VERBS
						vouloir → *voulu(e)(s)*
						avoir → *eu(e)(s)*
						voir → *vu(e)(s)*
						pouvoir → *pu*
						savoir → *su*
						boire → *bu(e)(s)*
						lire → *lu(e)(s)*
						croire → *cru(e)(s)*
						faire → *fait(e)(s)*
						dire → *dit(e)(s)*
						écrire → *écrit(e)(s)*
						mettre → *mis(e)(s)*
						prendre → *pris(e)(s)*
						être → *été*
						etc.

APPENDIX F
Il est... and *c'est*...

The following chart shows most of the major uses of *il est* and *c'est*.

il est	*c'est*
1. Followed by a noun with no modifier (often profession, nationality, or religion) *Il est français.* *Elles sont professeurs.*	1. Followed by a noun with a modifier *C'est un grand homme.* *Ce sont de bons professeurs.*
2. Followed by an adjective with a definite referent *Il est grand.*	2. Followed by an adjective with an indefinite referent *C'est facile.* (an idea or concept, not a specific noun)
3. Referring to a particular noun *Il est facile.* (for example, *le livre*)	3. Followed by a pronoun *C'est lui.*
4. In a prepositional phrase of location *Il est à Paris.* *Il est dans mon sac.*	4. In a prepositional phrase other than location *C'est à moi.* *C'est pour vous.*
5. In idioms and set expressions *Il est une heure.* (telling time)	5. In idioms and set expressions *C'est lundi.* *C'est demain le 23.* *Est-ce que...* (questions)

Il est is used to introduce a clause when the subject will be stated later in the sentence. *C'est* is used when the subject will not be stated.

Il est facile **de** faire cela.	It's easy to do that.
C'est facile **à** faire.	It's easy to do.

 QUICK CHECK

As a test, try to turn the sentence around.

"To do that is easy."

Since you can turn the sentence around, *il est* is correct.

"To do is easy."

Since this sentence makes no sense, *c'est* is used.

Cardinal numbers

Following are cardinal numbers in French, from 1 to 100 and beyond.

0	zéro	36	trente-six	72	soixante-douze
1	un	37	trente-sept	73	soixante-treize
2	deux	38	trente-huit	74	soixante-quatorze
3	trois	39	trente-neuf	75	soixante-quinze
4	quatre	40	quarante	76	soixante-seize
5	cinq	41	quarante et un	77	soixante-dix-sept
6	six	42	quarante-deux	78	soixante-dix-huit
7	sept	43	quarante-trois	79	soixante-dix-neuf
8	huit	44	quarante-quatre	80	quatre-vingts
9	neuf	45	quarante-cinq	81	quatre-vingt-un
10	dix	46	quarante-six	82	quatre-vingt-deux
11	onze	47	quarante-sept	83	quatre-vingt-trois
12	douze	48	quarante-huit	84	quatre-vingt-quatre
13	treize	49	quarante-neuf	85	quatre-vingt-cinq
14	quatorze	50	cinquante	86	quatre-vingt-six
15	quinze	51	cinquante et un	87	quatre-vingt-sept
16	seize	52	cinquante-deux	88	quatre-vingt-huit
17	dix-sept	53	cinquante-trois	89	quatre-vingt-neuf
18	dix-huit	54	cinquante-quatre	90	quatre-vingt-dix
19	dix-neuf	55	cinquante-cinq	91	quatre-vingt-onze
20	vingt	56	cinquante-six	92	quatre-vingt-douze
21	vingt et un	57	cinquante sept	93	quatre-vingt-treize
22	vingt-deux	58	cinquante-huit	94	quatre-vingt-quatorze
23	vingt-trois	59	cinquante-neuf	95	quatre-vingt-quinze
24	vingt-quatre	60	soixante	96	quatre-vingt-seize
25	vingt-cinq	61	soixante et un	97	quatre-vingt-dix-sept
26	vingt-six	62	soixante-deux	98	quatre-vingt-dix-huit
27	vingt-sept	63	soixante-trois	99	quatre-vingt-dix-neuf
28	vingt-huit	64	soixante-quatre	100	cent
29	vingt-neuf	65	soixante-cinq	200	deux cents
30	trente	66	soixante-six	201	deux cents un
31	trente et un	67	soixante-sept	1,000	mille
32	trente-deux	68	soixante-huit	2,000	deux mille
33	trente-trois	69	soixante-neuf	1,000,000	un million
34	trente-quatre	70	soixante-dix		
35	trente-cinq	71	soixante et onze		

The number 70 is literally "sixty and ten"; the number 80 is "four twenties."

Answer key

Nouns

A   1. l'   2. la   3. les   4. le   5. les   6. les   7. le   8. les   9. l'   10. la

B   1. un   2. une   3. des   4. une   5. une   6. des   7. un   8. une   9. des   10. un

C   1. un   2. le   3. de la   4. du   5. de   6. des   7. Les, la   8. Les   9. une, la   10. une, un

Pronouns

A   1. Je   2. elles   3. vous   4. tu   5. il   6. Nous   7. Ils   8. Elle   9. Je   10. tu

B   1. Elle le lit.   2. Nous voulons le louer.   3. Il la prend.   4. Ne les perds pas.
5. Elles l'écrivent.   6. Nettoyons-la.   7. Ils peuvent le comprendre.   8. Tu les copies.
9. Gardez-les.   10. Vous la vendez.

C   1. vous   2. m'   3. nous   4. me   5. te

D   1. Elles leur en envoient.   2. Je lui téléphone.   3. Donnez-leur-en.   4. Il y travaille.
5. En veux-tu?   6. Il le leur enseigne.   7. Il les y enseigne.   8. Nous leur en offrons.
9. Donnez-m'en, s'il vous plaît.   10. Je vais les y mettre.   11. Nous t'y voyons toujours.
12. La leur explique-t-elle?

E   1. moi   2. Eux   3. vous   4. Elle   5. Toi   6. lui   7. elles   8. nous

F   1. la sienne   2. la nôtre   3. les miens   4. les tiennes   5. le sien   6. la vôtre
7. les leurs   8. le leur

G   1. b   2. e   3. a   4. d   5. e   6. c   7. a   8. b

H   1. Ce livre-ci et celui-là.   2. Ma maison et celle de ma sœur.   3. Ces restaurants-ci sont
bons, mais ceux-là sont meilleurs.   4. Votre cours et celui que nous suivons sont
excellents.   5. Elle est celle qu'il aime.   6. Ces jardins-ci et ceux-là.   7. Veux-tu ces
pâtisseries-là ou celles-ci?   8. Nous pouvons prendre ma voiture. Celle de Marie n'est
pas assez grande.

I   1. À qui   2. Que   3. Qu'est-ce qu'   4. Laquelle   5. De quoi   6. Avec qui
7. À quoi   8. Lesquels   9. Qui (est-ce qui)   10. Qu'est-ce que   11. Qui est-ce que
12. Qu'est-ce qui   13. Pour qui   14. Duquel

Adjectives

A   1a. intéressant   1b. intéressante   1d. intéressantes   2b. blanche   2c. blancs
2d. blanches   3a. fier   3b. fière   3d. fières   4b. merveilleuse   4c. merveilleux
4d. merveilleuses   5a. gros   5b. grosse   5d. grosses   6a. heureux   6b. heureuse
6c. heureux   7b. active   7c. actifs   7d. actives   8b. nationale   8c. nationaux
8d. nationales   9b. italienne   9c. italiens   9d. italiennes   10b. légère   10c. légers
10d. légères

B   1. nouvelles   2. nouveau   3. nouvelle   4. nouvel   5. nouveaux   6. nouvel

C   1. bel   2. beau   3. belle   4. bel   5. beaux   6. belles

D   1. vieille   2. vieux   3. vieil   4. vieille   5. vieil   6. vieilles

E   1. un pauvre homme   2. une chère amie   3. un ancien général   4. une ville
ancienne   5. une grande femme   6. un homme pauvre   7. une (jeune) fille grande
8. une voiture chère

F   1. Jacques est plus intelligent que Marc.   2. Ma sœur est moins heureuse que mon frère.
3. C'est le meilleur livre de la bibliothèque.   4. Le métro est plus rapide que le bus.
5. C'est le pire étudiant du lycée.   6. Mon cours est moins intéressant que leur cours.

G   1. cet   2. Ces   3. Cette   4. ce   5. Cet   6. ce   7. Ces   8. Ces

H   1. son livre   2. mon école   3. sa maison   4. notre traduction   5. leurs jardins
6. tes idées   7. vos cahiers   8. mes devoirs   9. ton affiche   10. son histoire

I   1. Quelle   2. Quel   3. quel   4. Quel   5. Quels   6. Quelles   7. Quels   8. Quelle

Adverbs

A   1. facilement   2. activement   3. merveilleusement   4. bien   5. lentement
6. clairement   7. vivement   8. certainement   9. soigneusement   10. vaguement

Negatives

A   1. Il ne travaille pas.   2. Il ne travaille plus.   3. Il ne travaille jamais.   4. Personne
ne travaille.   5. Elle n'apprend rien.   6. Nous ne voyons ni Christine ni Marie.

Prepositions

A   1. en   2. en   3. à   4. au   5. à   6. aux   7. à la   8. en

B   1. à   2. X   3. X   4. de   5. de   6. à   7. de   8. X   9. X   10. de   11. à   12. de

Questions

A   1. Jean achète-t-il des livres?   2. Avons-nous dîné ici?   3. Suivez-vous cette route?
4. Les a-t-il pris?   5. Carole vous a-t-elle téléphoné?

Verbs

A 1. marchant, marché   2. choisissant, choisi   3. ayant, eu   4. descendant, descendu
5. lisant, lu   6. mentant, menti   7. étant, été   8. souriant, souri   9. balayant, balayé
10. nettoyant, nettoyé   11. achetant, acheté   12. préférant, préféré   13. prenant, pris
14. sachant, su   15. ouvrant, ouvert   16. réfléchissant, réfléchi   17. buvant, bu
18. faisant, fait   19. recevant, reçu   20. disant, dit   21. mettant, mis   22. pouvant, pu
23. voyant, vu   24. écrivant, écrit

B 1. marchent   2. choisissons   3. descends   4. ment   5. finit   6. sort   7. chantes
8. vend   9. cours   10. dors   11. louez   12. servent   13. réfléchissez   14. partent
15. rend

C 1. Où va-t-il? OR Où est-ce qu'il va?   2. Je marche toujours le matin.
3. Où travaillent-elles? OR Où est-ce qu'elles travaillent?   4. Nous attendons depuis
une heure.   5. Je ne sais pas où il est.   6. Washington, D.C. est la capitale des États-Unis.
7. Je pars pour Paris la semaine prochaine.   8. Il parle espagnol.

D 1. Il parlait avec sa fiancée.   2. Nous finissions notre travail.   3. Elle prenait un café.
4. J'attendais mes amis.   5. L'enfant dormait.   6. Nous étions pressés.   7. Tu vendais
ta maison.   8. Elle travaillait dans ce bureau.   9. Nous étudiions nos leçons.
10. Il fallait partir.   11. Ils allaient en ville.   12. Je faisais mes devoirs.   13. Tu écrivais
une lettre.   14. Vous lisiez beaucoup.   15. Je sortais.   16. Elle était en ville.
17. Le professeur effaçait le tableau.   18. Tu mangeais à une heure.

E 1. ira   2. aurai   3. prendrons   4. sortiras   5. passerai   6. choisirons   7. rendrez
8. devrons   9. enverrai   10. réussira   11. serez   12. pourront   13. faudra
14. arriveras   15. attendrez   16. finiront   17. nettoierons   18. achèteront

F 1. Nous allons sortir.   2. Elles vont arriver demain.   3. Il va venir avec eux.
4. Je vais monter.   5. Ils vont voir ce film.   6. Tu vas me téléphoner.   7. Vous allez
comprendre.   8. Nous allons être en retard.   9. Tu vas commander un thé.
10. Je vais passer te voir.

G 1. auraient   2. préférerais   3. jetterait   4. feraient   5. rendrions   6. choisiriez
7. verraient   8. enlèverais   9. balaierais   10. seraient

H 1. ont servi   2. a commencé   3. ai nagé   4. est entrée   5. a lavé   6. avons déjeuné
7. sont sortis   8. avez apporté   9. est mort   10. est née   11. avons pris   12. ont vendu
13. avez réfléchi   14. as organisé   15. sont retournées   16. se sont lavés
17. as demandé   18. as minci

I 1. Elle était déjà descendue.   2. J'avais déjà accepté.   3. Ils avaient déjà joué.
4. Elles étaient déjà rentrées.   5. Nous avions déjà parlé.   6. J'avais déjà téléphoné.
7. Ils étaient déjà partis.   8. Nous y avions déjà réfléchi.

J 1. sera arrivée   2. auras fini   3. aurai déjeuné   4. seront partis   5. aura décidé
6. serai rentré(e)

K 1. avions su, serions venu(e)s   2. aurait aidé, aviez demandé   3. ne l'aurait pas dit, avait
été   4. ne l'aurais pas fait, m'avait dit   5. avais fait, ne serais pas tombé(e)   6. avaient
travaillé, auraient réussi   7. avais été, aurais pu   8. aurais compris, avais fait

L 1. puisse   2. attende   3. veulent   4. saches   5. soit   6. aille   7. revient   8. fasse
9. mangions   10. boives   11. prennes   12. comprend   13. veniez   14. rendes
15. écrives

Using your French

A 1. Il y avait un chat gris sur une table ronde.   2. Il y avait un grand lit à côté d'une fenêtre ouverte.   3. Il y avait des tableaux obscurs sur un mur.   4. Il y avait une lampe éteinte près d'un fauteuil défoncé.   5. Il y avait des livres anciens sous un tapis usé.   6. Il y avait des chaussures déchirées dans un lavabo fêlé.   7. Il y avait un bruit étrange derrière une porte fermée.   8. Il y avait un homme endormi sur une chaise cassée.

B 1. Mettez la nouvelle imprimante sur le grand bureau.   2. Mettez les chaises autour de la table.   3. Mettez le poste de télé en face du canapé noir.   4. Mettez le fauteuil blanc devant la fenêtre ouverte.   5. Mettez les vêtements dans la penderie.   6. Mettez le gros frigo à côté de la cuisinière.   7. Mettez les assiettes cassées dans la poubelle vide.   8. Mettez la grosse lampe au sous-sol.   9. Mettez la corbeille à papier derrière la chaise bleue.   10. Mettez les boîtes fermées sous l'escalier.

C 1. Je me trouvais seule.   2. J'étais dans un champ.   3. Le ciel était gris.   4. Le vent soufflait.   5. Il commençait à pleuvoir.   6. Au loin on entendait des cris.   7. Moi, je pleurais.   8. La pluie me mouillait.   9. J'avais froid.   10. La terre tremblait.

D 1. Au huitième étage le facteur a apporté un colis pour mon ami Robert.   2. Au premier étage Marie Grimbert et son mari sont sortis à dix heures.   3. Au neuvième étage une vieille dame est tombée dans le couloir.   4. Au quatrième étage la police a frappé à la porte d'un appartement.   5. Au douzième étage Monsieur Garric n'est pas allé au travail aujourd'hui.   6. Au cinquième étage le plombier est arrivé chez les Doucet.   7. Au sixième étage Jacquot a sorti les ordures ménagères.   8. Au quinzième étage Mme Hardy a mis de nouveaux rideaux à sa fenêtre.   9. Au dixième étage la concierge a nettoyé le tapis.   10. Au deuxième étage des voleurs sont entrés dans l'appartement des Mercier.

E 1a. que Marie-Claire revienne.   1b. que Marie-Claire revient.   1c. que Marie-Claire revienne.   1d. que Marie-Claire revient/reviendra.   2a. qu'ils sont ponctuels.   2b. qu'ils soient ponctuels.   2c. qu'ils soient ponctuels.   2d. qu'ils sont ponctuels.   3a. qu'elle réponde à tous les messages.   3b. qu'elle réponde à tous les messages.   3c. qu'elle réponde à tous les messages.   3d. qu'elle répond à tous les messages.   4a. que vous sachiez la réponse.   4b. que vous sachiez la réponse.   4c. que vous savez la réponse.   4d. que vous savez la réponse.   5a. que tu réussisses à vendre ta voiture.   5b. que tu réussis à vendre ta voiture.   5c. que tu réussisses à vendre ta voiture.   5d. que tu réussis à vendre ta voiture.

F 1. Je veux dormir et je veux que les enfants dorment aussi.   2. Je préfère réfléchir et je préfère que tu réfléchisses aussi.   3. Il me faut le faire et il faut qu'ils le fassent aussi.   4. Il vaut mieux revenir et il vaut mieux qu'elle revienne aussi.   5. Vous voulez louer une voiture et vous voulez que nous louions une voiture aussi.   6. Nous sommes contents de pouvoir partir et nous sommes contents que notre ami puisse partir aussi.   7. Tu veux sortir et tu veux que je sorte aussi.   8. Nous désirons y aller et nous désirons que tu y ailles aussi.   9. J'aime mieux être ponctuel et j'aime mieux que vous soyez ponctuel aussi.   10. Je veux maigrir et je veux que mon copain maigrisse aussi.

G 1. Où est-ce que tu es allée hier?   2. Avec qui est-ce que tu y es allée?   3. À quelle heure est-ce qu'il est arrivé?   4. Qu'est-ce que tu as commandé?   5. Est-ce que tu as mangé quelque chose?   6. De quoi est-ce que vous avez parlé?   7. Pourquoi est-ce que vous n'avez pas dîné ensemble?   8. Quand est-ce que vous comptez vous revoir?

H 1. Quelle est votre adresse?   2. Où étiez-vous hier soir?   3. Pourquoi y êtes-vous allée?   4. Quel travail avez-vous fait?   5. Qui vous a vue à la bibliothèque?   6. Quel est son numéro de téléphone?   7. Quand avez-vous quitté la bibliothèque?   8. Où êtes-vous allée après?

I 1. Marc veut apprendre à parler japonais.   2. Louise et Léa essaient de trouver un travail.   3. Paul et Pierre s'intéressent voyager en Europe.   4. Ils commencent à chercher des billets d'avion.   5. Jacqueline préfère rester à la maison.   6. Arthur vient de trouver un nouvel appartement.   7. Les Gagnon invitent Géraldine à passer l'été dans leur chalet de montagne.   8. Mathilde suggère à ses amis d'aider les pauvres.

J 1. Il était neuf heures quinze quand il est sorti.   2. Il faisait beau quand Amélie est arrivée au bureau.   3. Il était tard quand la secrétaire est venue.   4. Il faisait froid dans le bureau quand les employés ont commencé à travailler.   5. Il était midi et demi quand je suis descendu(e) déjeuner.   6. Je mangeais quand il a commencé à pleuvoir.   7. J'étais tout(e) mouillé(e) quand je suis retourné(e) au bureau.   8. Les rues étaient sèches quand j'ai quitté le bureau.

K 1. Nous ne lui montrons pas nos courriels.   2. Je ne lui ai pas envoyé les documents.   3. Elle ne lui a pas dit son numéro de téléphone.   4. Ils ne lui ont pas rendu l'argent.   5. Il ne lui a pas offert une montre.   6. Il ne leur donne pas les médicaments.   7. Il ne leur a pas laissé son entreprise.   8. Il ne leur a pas vendu toute sa propriété.

L 1. Je ne sais pas s'il en achète.   2. Je ne sais pas s'il y passe ses vacances.   3. Je ne sais pas s'il y travaille.   4. Je ne sais pas si elle en envoie.   5. Je ne sais pas s'ils y sont.   6. Je ne sais pas si nous en avons signé.   7. Je ne sais pas s'il en a embauché.   8. Je ne sais pas si nous allons y organiser un dîner d'affaires.

M 1. Il faut le lui lire.   2. Nous devons leur en acheter.   3. Ils doivent leur en donner.   4. Nous allons les y emmener.   5. Marguerite peut vous en rapporter de France.   6. Je compte les lui prêter.   7. On doit lui en envoyer.   8. Je vais lui en préparer.

N 1. Je ne la trouve pas. / Cherche-la. Tu la trouveras.   2. Je ne le trouve pas. / Cherche-le. Tu le trouveras.   3. Je ne la trouve pas. / Cherche-la. Tu la trouveras.   4. Je ne les trouve pas. / Cherche-les. Tu les trouveras.   5. Je ne la trouve pas. / Cherche-la. Tu la trouveras.   6. Je ne les trouve pas. / Cherche-les. Tu les trouveras.   7. Je ne le trouve pas. / Cherche-le. Tu le trouveras.   8. Je ne les trouve pas. / Cherche-les. Tu les trouveras.

O 1. Julie veut travailler en France.   2. Samuel préfère rester aux États-Unis.   3. Mes cousins refusent d'aller en Espagne.   4. Mathieu continue à faire ses études à la Nouvelle-Orléans.   5. Pauline et son mari cherchent à trouver un logement au Mexique.   6. Camille réussit à trouver un poste à Londres.   7. Les Duhamel aiment passer l'hiver en Floride.   8. Isaac et moi, nous venons d'arriver au Havre.

P 1. J'irai au cinéma à moins que tu ne puisses pas m'accompagner.   2. J'expliquerai tout encore une fois pour que tu comprennes.   3. Nous sortirons bien qu'il ne fasse pas beau.   4. On partira avant qu'elle revienne.   5. Je resterai avec l'enfant jusqu'à ce qu'il s'endorme.   6. Nous réussirons à le faire pourvu que nous nous mettions à travailler.   7. Cet employé travaille peu sans que son chef s'en rende compte.   8. Je n'y vais pas de peur qu'il ne soit pas là.

Q 1. Ma mère fera le dîner.   2. Ma sœur et moi, nous laverons et sécherons la vaisselle.   3. Mon frère regardera un match à la télé.   4. Mon père lira le journal.   5. Mes grands-parents joueront aux cartes.   6. Ma cousine viendra nous voir.   7. Les voisins prendront le dessert avec nous.   8. Ma tante verra un film.   9. Moi, je serai contente de parler avec tout le monde.   10. Nous pourrons nous amuser ensemble.

R 1. Justine monterait une affaire.   2. Mes voisins prendraient la retraite.   3. Claude ferait un voyage en Asie.   4. Moi, j'achèterais une maison à Tahiti.   5. Mes grands-parents seraient contents.   6. Toi, tu irais habiter au bord de la mer.   7. Nous voudrions aider notre famille.   8. Moi, je pourrais acheter une Lamborghini.   9. Philippe paierait ses dettes.   10. On dînerait dans les meilleurs restaurants.

S 1. Lucie ne sortira jamais avec Mathieu.   2. Mon oncle et ma tante ne reviendront pas de France cette année.   3. Tu ne prêteras plus d'argent à Michel.   4. Nous ne recevrons rien pour notre anniversaire.   5. Vous ne verrez personne au bureau.   6. Je ne ferai plus les courses le matin.   7. Émile et Jacqueline n'iront jamais plus en vacances ensemble.   8. Personne ne complétera le projet aujourd'hui.   9. Nous ne saurons jamais ce qui est arrivé.   10. Je ne serai plus dans le même rayon que toi.

T 1. Si on préparait l'ordre du jour, on ne perdrait pas tant de temps.   2. Si tout le monde ne parlait pas pendant la réunion, on avancerait assez vite.   3. Si on avait toutes les données, on pourrait proposer les solutions nécessaires.   4. Si notre directeur parlait clairement, les employés comprendraient les problèmes.   5. Si l'entreprise servait le déjeuner, il ne faudrait pas interrompre la réunion.   6. Si les employés avaient les documents, ils seraient préparés.   7. Si nous avions les comptes-rendus, nous saurions combien on a vendu.   8. Si la réunion était bien organisée, il ne nous faudrait pas rester jusqu'à neuf heures du soir.

U 1. Si nous n'étions pas allés à la plage, nous nous serions amusés.   2. Si l'hôtel avait été propre, on ne se serait pas senti mal a l'aise.   3. Si les restaurants n'avaient pas été mauvais, je ne serais pas tombé malade.   4. S'il n'avait pas plu tous les jours, on aurait pu nager.   5. Si le cinéma n'aurait pas été fermé, on aurait vu des films.   6. Si je n'avais pas oublié mon livre, j'aurais pu lire.   7. Si nos amis étaient venus avec nous, les vacances n'auraient pas été désagréables.   8. Si nous n'y étions pas restés trop longtemps, on ne se serait pas ennuyés.

V 1. Nous cherchons un chef de bureau qui connaisse la bureautique.   2. On voudrait trouver un secrétaire qui sache écrire en allemand et en anglais.   3. Il nous faut des représentants qui puissent voyager souvent.   4. Nous avons besoin d'une banque qui ait des succursales en Asie.   5. Je cherche un directeur qui comprenne les nouvelles technologies.   6. Il nous faut un fournisseur qui garantisse la sécurité de notre réseau.   7. Nous voulons embaucher des employés qui fassent un bon travail.   8. Nous cherchons de nouveaux marchés qui soient rentables.

W 1. Non, personne ne va donner un travail à Emma.   2. Non, Philippe n'a jamais beaucoup à faire.   3. Non, Jacques n'a jamais de très bonnes notes.   4. Non, Léonie ne trouve rien d'intéressant.   5. Non, Juliette n'achète ni une Ferrari ni une Lamborghini.   6. Non, Florian ne parle avec personne en ce moment.   7. Non, Stella n'est plus à la campagne.   8. Non, Matthieu n'est pas encore arrivé.

X   1. Quand nous sommes arrivé(e)s à l'aéroport, l'avion était déjà parti.   2. Quand Luc s'est levé, nous avions déjà servi le petit déjeuner.   3. Quand Lucie a envoyé sa demande d'emploi, l'entreprise avait déjà embauché quelqu'un.   4. Quand Maurice a laissé le pourboire, Pierre avait déjà payé l'addition.   5. Quand les invités ont frappé à la porte, Monique s'était déjà habillée.   6. Quand le taxi est arrivé, Christine et son mari avaient déjà fait leurs valises.   7. Quand le chef m'a appelé, j'avais déjà fini mon travail. 8. Quand les employés sont venus, on avait déjà fermé le bureau.

Y   1. Tous les employés ont été invités.   2. Les billets de train ont été achetés par la secrétaire.   3. Les réservations ont été faites par le chef de bureau.   4. L'itinéraire a été décidé par les employés.   5. Un guide a été embauché par une agence de voyage. 6. Des activités ont été organisées par l'hôtel.   7. Des rencontres professionnelles ont été arrangées par l'entreprise.   8. Des visites intéressantes ont été programmées.

Z   1. —Quels gants achetez-vous? —Ceux qui sont en solde.   2. —Quels documents lisez-vous? —Ceux qui étaient sur mon bureau.   3. —Quelle voiture préférez-vous? —Celle de mon oncle.   4. —Quelles villes visitez-vous? —Celles qui sont présentées sur mon itinéraire.   5. —Quelle maison vendez-vous? —Celle de notre quartier. 6. —Quels employés embauchez-vous? —Ceux qui parlent au moins deux langues étrangères.   7. —Quels livres empruntez-vous? —Ceux de mes amis. 8. —Quels tableaux voulez-vous regarder? —Ceux qui sont dans le musée d'art.

AA   1. —Est-ce que cette église est plus ancienne que l'autre? —Oui, c'est l'église la plus ancienne de la ville.   2. —Est-ce que ce magasin est plus cher que l'autre? —Oui, c'est le magasin le plus cher du quartier.   3. —Est-ce que ce restaurant est meilleur que l'autre? —Oui, c'est le meilleur restaurant de la rue.   4. —Est-ce que ces industries sont plus importantes que les autres? —Oui, ce sont les industries les plus importantes de la région. 5. —Est-ce que ces écoles sont plus connues que les autres? —Oui, ce sont les écoles les plus connues du pays.   6. —Est-ce que ce paysage est plus admiré que l'autre? —Oui, c'est le paysage le plus admiré de la province.   7. —Est-ce que ce fleuve est plus large que l'autre? —Oui, c'est le fleuve le plus large du Midi.   8. —Est-ce que ces ports sont plus actifs que les autres? —Oui, ce sont les ports les plus actifs du continent.

BB   1. Le vieil homme marche lentement.   2. Chloé participe activement à la création du site Web.   3. Noah répond vivement.   4. Le jeune couple vit heureusement.   5. Tout le monde se promène agréablement.   6. Je me lève rapidement.   7. Léa sort furieusement. 8. Les enfants chantent doucement.

CC   1. Pierre et Lucie sont revenus d'Europe à neuf heures.   2. J'ai répondu à quarante-cinq courriels.   3. Émile a dépensé huit cents euros au grand magasin.   4. Ma tante Adèle a gagné quinze mille euros à la loterie.   5. Sophie a lu deux cent soixante pages. 6. Robert a parlé cinquante minutes au téléphone.   7. Le restaurant du coin a servi trois cent soixante-dix clients.   8. Nous avons connu des touristes de vingt-et-un pays différents.

DD   1. Ils doutent que nous puissions les aider.   2. Nous sommes sûrs de pouvoir les aider. 3. Je ne crois pas que vous acceptiez l'offre d'emploi.   4. Vous voulez accepter l'offre d'emploi.   5. J'ai peur qu'il (ne) soit en retard.   6. Il a peur d'être en retard. 7. Elle est ravi que tu viennes.   8. Tu es content de venir.

EE 1. —Notre ville est plus élégante que Paris. —Pas vrai. Paris est aussi élégant que notre ville. 2. —Philippe est plus intelligent que Marc. —Pas vrai. Marc est aussi intelligent que Philippe. 3. —Ce roman est plus passionnant que l'autre roman. —Pas vrai. L'autre roman est aussi passionnant que ce roman. 4. —Cette chanteuse française est plus célèbre que la chanteuse canadienne. —Pas vrai. La chanteuse canadienne est aussi célèbre que la chanteuse française. 5. —Cette tarte au citron est meilleure que la tarte aux poires. —Pas vrai. La tarte aux poires est aussi bonne que cette tarte au citron. 6. —Cet appartement est plus cher que cette maison. —Pas vrai. Cette maison est aussi chère que cet appartement. 7. —Élisabeth est plus charmante qu'Inès. —Pas vrai. Inès est aussi charmante qu'Élisabeth. 8. —Cette étudiante est plus gentille que le professeur. —Pas vrai. Le professeur est aussi gentil que cette étudiante.

FF 1. Il se brosse les dents. 2. Sa sœur Camille se réveille à sept heures. 3. Antoine se rase et prend une douche. 4. Sa mère se lave la tête. 5. Tout le monde s'habille vite. 6. Ils se préparent pour la journée. 7. Antoine et Camille s'asseyent pour le petit déjeuner. 8. Ils se disent au revoir.

GG 1. Vous vous intéressez aux projets. 2. Vous ne vous énervez pas facilement. 3. Vous vous passionnez pour les idées. 4. Vous ne vous fâchez pas avec les collègues. 5. Vous vous adressez poliment à tout le monde. 6. Vous vous souciez de la qualité du travail. 7. Vous vous donnez la peine d'apprendre des nouvelles technologies. 8. Vous ne vous en allez pas du bureau avant cinq heures.

HH 1. —Les enfants n'ont pas fait leurs devoirs. —Pourquoi est-ce qu'ils ne les ont pas faits? 2. —Mes parents ont acheté une nouvelle voiture. —Où est-ce qu'ils l'ont achetée? 3. —J'ai reçu deux messages mystérieux. —À quelle heure est-ce que tu les a reçus? 4. —J'ai perdu mes clés. —Quand est-ce que tu les a perdues? 5. —Nous avons regardé les actualités. —Avec qui est-ce que vous les avez regardées? 6. —Paul a retrouvé Agathe et Eugénie. —Où est-ce qu'il les a retrouvées? 7. —Les Garnier ont vendu leur maison. —À qui est-ce qu'ils l'ont vendue? 8. —Aurélie a vu le nouveau film italien. —Avec qui est-ce qu'elle l'a vu?